ISBN: 9781314824032

Published by:
HardPress Publishing
8345 NW 66TH ST #2561
MIAMI FL 33166-2626

Email: info@hardpress.net
Web: http://www.hardpress.net

FLORA ORCADENSIS

M. SPENCE, F.E.I.S.

FLORA ORCADENSIS

CONTAINING THE FLOWERING PLANTS

ARRANGED ACCORDING TO THE
NATURAL ORDERS

BY

MAGNUS SPENCE, F.E.I.S.
DEERNESS

AND

THE MOSSES

BY

LIEUT.-COLONEL JAMES GRANT, V.D.
J.P., L.R.C.P. AND S. EDIN., F.S.A. SCOT.
OF STROMNESS

With Maps and Portraits

KIRKWALL
D. SPENCE, BROAD STREET
1914

FOREWORD.

A FLORA of Orkney has long been greatly desired by those who take an interest in the wild flowers of these islands. For over two centuries the only available information on the subject has consisted of various lists more or less incomplete and usually buried in periodicals inaccessible to the general reader.

The appearance of Mr Spence's "Flora" is especially opportune at the present time, when Nature Study is one of the educational fashions of the day, and when agricultural science is receiving so much attention.

This book is the result of many years of careful observation and research, and the author has spared neither time nor trouble in making his work as full and accurate as possible. Having lived for many years in Stenness and then in Deerness, Mr Spence has had exceptional opportunities of investigating the plants indigenous to both the West and East Mainland, while, during his holidays, he has carefully examined the vegetation of the other more important islands. His long and intimate acquaintance with Orkney has thus eminently fitted him for the compilation of this " Flora." His trained faculty for observation in other branches of science, notably meteorology, combined with an enthusiastic love of and sympathy with Nature, constitute him a botanist of the first order, and those who are interested in the natural history of Orkney have great reason to congratulate themselves that such a man has, during a very busy life, found time to undertake this work.

Mr Spence has increased the value of his " Flora" by incorporating the remarks of specialists on the doubtful or " critical " plants which have come under his notice.

The addition of Dr Grant's " List of Mosses " will be of service to those interested in that beautiful but too little known class.

W. IRVINE FORTESCUE, M.D.

CONTENTS

PORTRAITS AND MAPS.

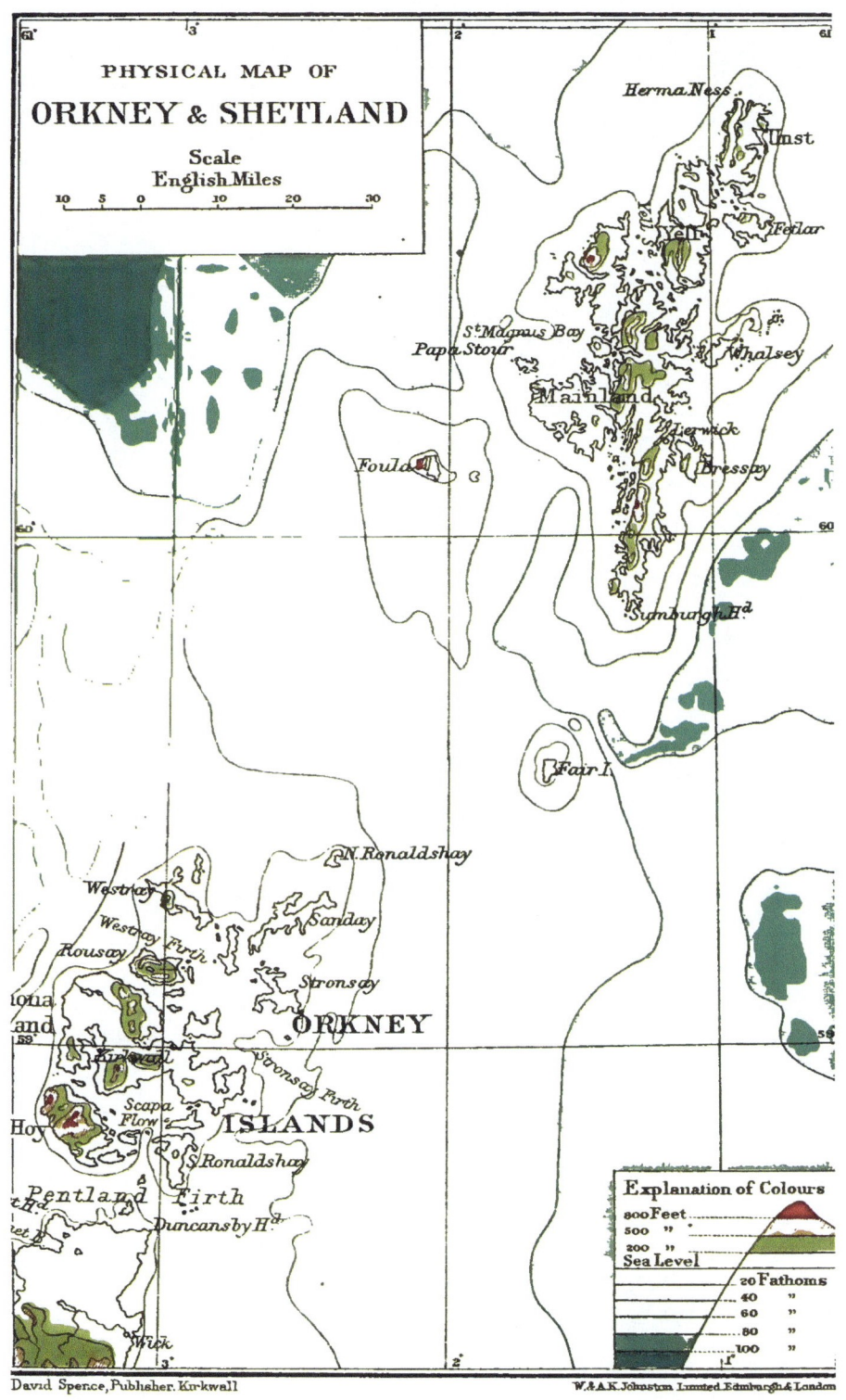

PHYSICAL MAP OF

ORKNEY & SHETLAND

Scale
English Miles

10 5 0 10 20 30

Herma Ness

Unst

Yell

Fetlar

St Magnus Bay

Papa Stour

Whalsey

Mainland

Lerwick

Bressay

Foula

Sumburgh Hd

Fair I.

N. Ronaldshay

Westray

Sanday

Westray Firth

Rousay

Stronsay

ORKNEY

Kirkwall

Stronsay Firth

Scapa
Flow

Hoy

ISLANDS

S. Ronaldshay

Pentland Firth

Duncansby Hd

Wick

Explanation of Colours

800 Feet
500   "
200   "
Sea Level

20 Fathoms
40   "
60   "
80   "
100   "

David Spence, Publisher, Kirkwall   W. & A.K. Johnston Limited, Edinburgh & London

FLORA ORCADENSIS.

INTRODUCTORY.

THE Science of Botany seeks to elucidate plant
life in its various forms. The study of this
science in its fullest sense embraces plant mor-
phology, anatomy, physiology, ecology, palæobotany,
pathology, and systematic botany. Only a few
botanists have been able to devote the time necessary to master all these branches of the subject.
Many people study the subject as a hobby, and
find it one of the most delightful and exhilarating
of studies, as it takes its votaries far afield in the
bracing air and sunshine of our heaths, moors, and
sea-sides. In fact, the one branch of botany which
suits the holiday excursionist is systematic botany.
It classifies all plant life and elaborates schemes of
relationship whereby the affinities of plants to one
another are shown. The essential study in modern
systematic botany is by a comparison of the processes of growth and development. We can thus
arrange plants in groups according to relationships

which enable the student to find without much
trouble the characteristics of the individuals of the
same order, and to place them in the families
assigned to them by the great masters of the subject
as Linnæus, Hooker, Boswell, &c. Some people may
consider that the classification of plants is simply
the process of cataloguing them, or collecting and
preserving them in the herbarium of the collector.
It is true that many take no more interest in the
subject than to collect ; but we must not forget that
one of the most interesting studies in systematic
botany is that of the relationship and possible origin
of the numerous species which come under observation. Such a study gives one an insight into the
whole scheme of plant evolution.

Most of our earliest botanists devoted much time
to systematic botany. No real progress could be
made so long as the innumerable genera and species
remained unclassified. Systematic botany is the
frame-work on which Botany as a science has been
built up. Animals, birds, fossils, and rocks have each
received this systematic study. Linnæus was the
first to bring order out of chaos and to name plants
according to a uniform system. He instituted the
present binominal nomenclature, in which every plant
has a generic name like a surname, and a specific
name in the form of an adjective, either in Latin or
some modern Latinised form.

The present " Flora" is written with the view of
meeting a much felt want. To the schoolmaster it
should form a handy book of reference when pupils
bring to him—as I am told they do—all the

unknown plants met with on their daily rounds to and from school. Under present school requirements the teacher is expected to take the older pupils for excursions, at least in the neighbourhood of the school, to familiarise them with the local flora. When their interest is stimulated and a love of flowers instilled, they bring specimens to him to identify. With this handbook and some standard " Flora of Great Britain," he should have no difficulty in giving the required information.

The " Memorandum of Nature Study" issued by the Education Department states :—" Where practicable, rambles for the study of things in their ordinary surroundings will naturally be frequent, so that each pupil, even in a large school, may be able to participate in as many as possible during the session." " The continuous study of a living plant in its natural environment, accompanied by careful, dated records, of its growth, development, and change throughout the successive seasons of the year, forms an exceptionally interesting and valuable exercise."

Few will deny the great educative value of a study of botany; but in rural districts its economic value is perhaps even more apparent. Much of the information published at the present day for the use of the agriculturist on the crops which he grows every year and the injurious weeds which he tries to extirpate from his fields, is simply unintelligible to the average farmer, owing to his lack of even a rudimentary knowledge of botany. As an illustration of what I mean, I once attended a lecture on grasses by a lecturer from an Agricultural College. He began by assuming that every farmer knew the common grasses. He talked learnedly on the subject without more than five per cent. being able to follow him. So long as he talked of rye-grass, cock's-foot-grass, and clover, which they all knew, they were interested and followed the lecturer with eager attention; but when he proceeded to treat of the less common grasses, such as meadow-fescue, sheep's-fescue, &c., which very few of them knew, they were hopelessly bewildered. After the lecture was over, I suggested that a few specimens and diagrams would have enabled the farmer to become familiar with these grasses. "It never occurred to me," he said, "that these practical farmers did not know the common grasses. I have not only diagrams at home but specimens of all the plants I have been treating of. It seemed superfluous for me to bring specimens of the plants over which they tread every day."

Whoever desires to possess a knowledge of botany should first learn to identify the common plants in his own district; but even this much can hardly be done without having first mastered a working know-ledge of the rudiments of the science, including roots, stems, leaves, flowers, stamens, pistils, seed-vessels, &c. Given this elementary knowledge of botany, he is then in a position to understand the methods of botanical classification, and, with the assistance of a good book on systematic botany, to put each plant which comes under his observation into its proper class. The study of botany on these lines may not only be of great practical value to the agriculturist, but it adds also to the interests and pleasures of life. One who is ignorant of the floral treasures over which he treads in his daily walks or rounds of duty, has missed one of the most satisfying influences towards the realisation of that mental calm and inspiration which useful knowledge brings.

TOPOGRAPHY.

The Orkney Islands form a distinct group which is detached from the mainland of Scotland to the south and the Shetland Islands to the north. Broughness, in South Ronaldshay, the most southerly of the group, is about $7\frac{1}{4}$ miles from Duncansby Head, in Caithness ; while North Ronaldshay, the most northerly, is about 50 miles from Dunrossness, in Shetland. The Orkneys form an entity botanically. The group consists of 29 inhabited and 38 uninhabited islands. These small, uninhabited islands are botanically of very little interest. They are surf-washed, and the flowering plants and grasses found on them are hardy perennials little affected by the wash and spray of the sea. Many of them are interesting to the student of botany in so far as they have shown their adaptability to develop characteristics which fit them for their particular kind of development. Among these may be mentioned *Euphrasia maritima, matricaria maritima, Plantago maritima*, &c. The group is included within latitude 58°46' and 59°22' north and longitude 2°22' to 3°25' west. Of all the islands, the most interesting is Hoy, with its sheltered valleys, rocky

recesses, gullies, and corries, and its Meadow of the
Kame, forming a well-sheltered area with interesting
gorges leading to the higher grounds.   The most
noteworthy hill is the Ward, Hoy, rising to 1565
feet, with its hammars—exposed rocky ledges—about
half-way up, or probably a little less.   The hills and
sheltered valleys in Walls are also botanically interesting.   It is in these two localities, forming one
island, that most of our alpine plants are found.
The next highest hills are in Orphir and Rousay—
the Ward of the former rises to 881 feet, and
Blotchnie of the latter to 821 feet.

When considering the altitude at which a particular plant is likely to be found, latitude also has
to be taken into account.   For instance, I find that
Thalictrum alpina grows in several places in Orkney
within 100 feet above sea-level—near Hobbister,
Stenness; Scockness, Rousay; and elsewhere.   I have
found *Draba incana* at the Hammars of Syradale,
Firth, not more than 400 feet above sea-level ; and
again on Blotchnie, 800 feet high.   *Silene acaulis*
grows at the Hammars of Ward Hill, Hoy, 600 feet
high ; and on Skea Hill, Westray, only 250 feet
high.   Then *Carex rigida* grows near the top of
Ward Hill, Hoy ; but I found one plant on Kirbuster
Hill, Birsay, 335 feet high.   If we compare these
with the limiting altitudes given in Dr Whyte's
" Flora of Perthshire," we find that *Thalictrum
alpina* has its lowest limit of 950 feet in Atholl.
Draba incana has a limit of 1000 feet in Atholl;
and *Silene acaulis* has its lowest limit of 1200 feet
in Breadalbane.   The middle of Perth lies in latitude

56°30′, and Orkney in 59°, a difference of 2½°. Whilst some plants show a wider range than others, we are within the mark when we take it that there is a difference of 600 feet in range above sea-level between the same plants in Perth and Orkney, or 240 feet for every degree.

As our winter temperature is higher than that of Perth, and our sunshine little less, the difference in range of plants is solely due to the difference in summer temperature. The following statement shows this difference in temperature for four months :—

	Perth.	Deerness, Orkney.
January	37·3	39·0
April	45·1	42·4
July	58·7	54·2
September	53·3	51·5

The comparison of temperatures shows that Orkney is nearly 2° milder in winter and 4½° colder in midsummer than Perth. This summer temperature is the factor which determines the great difference in the altitude at which the same plant is found in different localities. The mean annual rainfall for Orkney is 36·65 inches, and for the city of Perth, 32·04 ; but for Ochtertyre, Perthshire, it is 41·42. The mean annual hours of sunshine for Orkney are 1185, and for Aberdeen and Fort Augustus—the nearest available sunshine stations to Perth—respectively 1401 and 907.

The statement below gives the monthly and annual means for temperature, sunshine, and rainfall for Orkney :—

	Mean Temperature. 1871-1905.		Mean Hours Sunshine. 1880-1907.		Mean Rainfall. 1841-1907.
January........	39·0	....	29·7	....	3·72
February......	38·5	....	55·5	....	3·05
March..........	39·3	....	101·1	....	2·82
April.....	42·4	....	154·1	....	1·99
May.............	46·4	....	178·5	....	1·81
June	51·3	....	160·9	....	1·97
July.............	54·2	....	141·3	....	2·57
August.........	54·0	....	121·8	....	3·01
September	51·5	....	108·8	....	3·09
October........	46·4	....	75·5	.. ..	4·43
November.....	42·4	....	36·5	....	3·97
December	39·9	....	20·8	....	4·21
Mean...	45·4	Total...	1184·5	Total...	36·65

These statistics do not help us much, as the variations in temperature, rainfall, and sunshine in different altitudes in Perthshire itself is as great as between the north and south of Scotland. Neither in Orkney nor in Perth do plants in normal seasons suffer from drought. The rainfall is well distributed in both. April, May, and June are the driest months in Orkney, but even during that period there is no lack of moisture. Sunshine is, after water, temperature, and soil, the most important factor in plant life. Very few county floras have been written for the north of Scotland. This is why we have chosen the "Flora of Perthshire" as a model with which to make comparisons. It was edited by Professor James Trail, F.R.S., F.L.S., of Aberdeen, whose well-known abilities and position are a guarantee of the thoroughness and reliability of the work.

NATURAL SELECTION.

The flora of a scattered group of islands is more interesting than that of a compact area of the same size. Comparative isolation reduces the risk of cross-fertilisation, and tends to give each species more scope to develop new characters in keeping with its environment. No part of botany is more interesting than the manner in which plants adapt themselves to their environment. One result which comes out with sufficient clearness from recent investigation is the great amount of variability there is in plants. Under moist conditions, a plant tends to develop hairiness, which protects the stomata from the entrance of water, thereby enabling the plant to thrive better than those not so protected. When this additional structure has developed, the plant is better able to surmount this peculiarity of climate. This characteristic developes healthier plants, which are consequently selected by Nature to an abundant growth. This is natural selection. Darwin says :—" As many more individuals of each species are born than can possibly survive, and as consequently there is a frequent, recurring struggle for existence, it follows that any being, if it vary, however slightly, in any manner profitable to itself, under the complex and varying conditions of life will have a better chance of surviving, and thus be *naturally selected*. From the strong principle of inheritance, any selected variety will tend to propagate its new and modified form. This preservation of favourable individual

differences and variations, and the destruction of
those which are injurious, I have called 'Natural
Selection, or the Survival of the Fittest.'"

Now if we take *Jasione montana*, or sheep's-bit,
as we find it in Eday, North Ronaldshay, and Fair
Isle, we shall see that Natural Selection is fitting
it to develop, in time, a new variety. Here are
three islands so remote from one another that if
some characteristic, such as increased hairiness, were
developed in one island it would diffuse its properties
among the individual plants of that island ; but no
communication with the other islands, either by
wind, waves, or insects is possible, owing to the
swift currents intervening. We find, as indicated in
the plant list under this particular plant, two peculiarities that through time will no doubt develop into
varieties. Then there is *Primula scotica*, isolated
into little patches here and there throughout the
Orkneys. One day, while wandering through St.
Andrews, I found a specimen which differed so much
from others of its kindred that I hardly knew it.
Growing on a small brae composed of nothing but
black, soft peat, it had unusually developed flower-
stalks, elongated petioles, and narrow leaves. The
difference from the type I at once set down to its
peaty habitat. Some time after, in the same neighbourhood, I found some *Primula* in a stiff clay,
bearing the same characteristics. This no doubt
revealed a transition stage, owing to environment.
It had travelled one stage on its way to a new
variety of plant. One interesting feature of plant
life is noticeable in North Ronaldshay. This island

is flat and raised very little above sea-level. Near the lighthouse on the north end is a bit of natural heath on which are found a few plants, which were doubtless more abundant before the extensive culti- vation of pasture-land. Some of these were difficult to name off-hand, as they presented unnatural appear- ances. St. John's wort—*Hypericum pulchrum*—was so prostrated by exposure to high winds that at first it looked like a new variety. Then *Potentilla tor- mentilla* had the same appearance, being flattened to the earth as if it were a creeping plant. This was more prominent there than elsewhere ; but through- out the islands the evidence of strong prevailing winds is clearly visible. On all the hills, especially on the west and north-west sides, the heather is prostrated in the direction of the prevailing winds.

There are two temperature problems which are ready to upset the calculations of a botanist. Our winter climate is milder than that of any other county in Scotland, and our summer is colder than any other—Shetland excepted, whose flora our owr very much resembles. *Veronica decussata*, an ever- green, grows well when sheltered from high winds. The winter of 1911 was mild and free from the high winds of former years. Two plants which had grown into bushes of over four feet in my garden produced one year many perfect flowers in January. The following year they were again in a well- advanced state when a continuance of gales for about four days blasted the buds ready to burst. *Fuchsia Magellanica* flowers well in Orkney, and in July is covered with its red and purple bell-flowers. These bushes are often used for hedges and sides of walks. One of our prettiest wild-flowers is fox-glove, *Digitalis purpurea*, which grows well in ditches and under the shelter of earthen dykes. It grows best, however, where there is rank vegetation surrounding it. These old withered grasses and flower-stalks seem to protect its roots and buds, especially in early spring ; when exposed it dies.

The most interesting features of a district to a field-botanist, especially in an exposed, treeless county like Orkney, are its corries and burns, in which shelter is provided for some of the rarer plants. There are many such shelter spots in Hoy and Walls ; a few are found, too, on the Mainland. One of the most interesting walks, from a botanical point of view, can be had by following the bed of the Burn of Syradale between Firth and Harray. A few fine rose bushes grow near the lower end of the burn at the foot of the steep declivity. Farther up on its rocky ledges grow plants of *Draba incana ;* while on crossing the peaty hill towards Redland there is abundance of *Scirpus pauciflora.* Then, on descending the other side, are some ferns—*Lastrea æmula* —and large specimens of *Lastrea dilatata.* In the same locality is to be found that graceful and beautiful plant, *Circæa alpina.* The Meadow of the Kame, with its connecting gullies leading to the hills outside, is the home of the filmy fern and of the rare *Saxifraga stellaris.* The Burn of Berriedale, with its tributaries, especially those on the west, gives shelter to an interesting group, where on the scree, in the widened bed of the stream, there is a varied and luxuriant growth of *valarian*, tall grasses, and small trees, *e.g.*, the rowan tree, black birch, and poplar. In the East Mainland there are no deep gorges to form homes for ferns and rare plants. In the neighbourhood of Græmeshall and St. Mary's are two miniature lochs where a few interesting specimens are to be found. *Scirpus tabernæmontani,* in Græmeshall Loch ; *Sium angustifolium,* in the burn leading to St. Mary's Loch ; and *Potamogeton pussilus,* in the same loch, are a few of the rarer plants. Then in a boggy meadow below Ocilster, in Holm, called the Trout-bog, grows the rare plant, *Lemna minor,* floating in still pools without roots of any kind to hold it *in situ.* One of the most interesting peat bogs is that of the White Moss, St. Andrews, where *Drosera rotundifolia* and *D. anglica* grow in great abundance. The Orkney flora would be monotonous and common-place if it were not for the sea with its crags and sandy beaches, its sand dunes and salt marshes, its muddy bays and burn mouths. Then large inland sheets of water, like Lochs Stenness and Harray, have plant associations peculiar to each. Large stretches of sandy pasture-land, known as links, have many plants not met with elsewhere, such as *Carex incurva, Carex arenaria, Senecio jacobæa,* and *Thalictrum minus,* var. *dunense.*

To one whose daily work confines him inside the four walls of a room, or amid the noise and bustle of a town, the privilege of spending a few hours every week with Nature is one of the most exhilarating out-door pleasures one can enjoy. The blue sky above, the green turf beneath, the charm of listening to the choirs untrained and natural, and the sweet perfume of the fragrant flowers, are delights which for the time being please the senses and charm the mind. When one is in sweet converse with Nature, one desires to be alone, free from the distractions of every-day life and work, and one's whole being concentrated on the activities which the display of flowers and the songs of birds call forth. One's whole soul likes then to dwell apart and ponder over the mysteries of Nature. Here is a flower which one did not expect to find in this locality. Why is it here? Is it developing any new characteristics not found in the type as a result of growth in a new environment? Here comes the busy bees. What are their favourite flowers to-day? How busy they are! Moths, too, are busy in the twilight. Do they, as scientists tell us, gather honey only from the fragrant flowers? And is it true that most of the flowers they frequent are colourless? They are attracted, it is said, by the perfume, and need no colour to please the eye —the white campion, the yellow-whitish primrose and the grass of Parnassus are more prized by them than the highly-coloured red campion, the heather bell, and the purple clover. Nature's diverse workers never rest—the bees by day and the moths by night, the former fascinated by gay colours, the latter by sweet perfume. Then the black-headed gull comes forth for his supper, well knowing that the moth which he relishes is on the hunt for honey. Nature is the great theatre in which, guided by instinct, **bird, beast, and insect play their part.** Birds, impelled by hunger, wage incessant war on the insect world ; insects draw their sustenance mostly from plants ; all the phases of animal life are mutually interdependent.

EXCURSIONS.

No doubt all botanists who ever shouldered a vasculum can recall many pleasant walks in the fields and many delightful incidents, which still fire the imagination—new flowers added to the herbarium, a long-looked-for friend found, or a curious abnormity discovered. Probably one of the greatest pleasures is to get into a well-sheltered crannie with an abundance of ferns. Plants and grasses hide among the ferns ; smaller and more delicate ferns among the more robust, and behind all tender flowerets almost afraid to open their eyes on the blaze of the blighting sun. I shall make my meaning more real if I describe one or two pleasant botanical trips. One of these I have reason to remember on account of the fatigue of the long walk, as I had only recently recovered from a severe attack of influenza. An excursion to Rousay by steamer was advertised. *Pyrola rotundifolia* was the object of attraction, which hitherto I had sought in vain. I passed up the burn near Trumland House (then the residence of the late General Burroughs), on the grounds of which several interesting plants are to be seen. Out on the peat moor in the valley I encountered a pair of long-eared owls which were seized with paroxysms of distress, or, more probably, ill-temper, at unwonted intrusion. Their actions guided me to a pair of young ones, which were so far advanced as to be able to fly short distances. After essaying what was no doubt their first flight, I handled them to see what the parents would do. To my disappointment both winged their flight to a short distance to view the proceedings. When the young were again set free the parents resumed their wonted fortitude. My sole guide to the whereabouts of this plant was that reference to it in Tudor's " The Orkneys and Shetland," in which he speaks of it as growing " near the Goukheads, where the Sourin Burn flows from the Muckle Water." While climbing the intervening hill, I found for the first time *Alchemilla vulgaris*, var. *filicaulis ;* and on the top of the hill *vaccinium myrtillus*, var. *microphylla*, previously reported from Shetland by Mr Beeby, a gentleman who had made a special botanical study of the plants of Shetland. On descending the hill on the other side, I found near the *hags* a glorious display of scores of *Pyrola rotundifolia* in full flower. The dark-brown heather served as a back-ground for the lovely waxen pink and white blossoms, which grew in slightly waving racemes so far apart as to enhance the beauty of the scene. Eager to touch yet loth to destroy, I lay down amid the heather and admired the picture. It is, I think, without exaggeration, the prettiest flower in Orkney.

From there I rounded the Muckle Water and climbed the Ward Hill; but before Trumbland Pier was reached aching limbs reminded me that the task had been overdone. The good luck which

crowned my efforts, combined with the genial sunshine and bracing air of that memorable occasion,
is representative of many other pleasant outings of
this kind. There is another side to the shield. One
illustration will suffice. I left Kirkwall one morning
by the Stromness coach for Bigswell Hill, Stenness.
The weather forecasts of that morning were falsified.
Proceeding by way of the hills near Hobbister, Stenness, I took a bee-line for the Bigswell Hills, and on
the way thither saw nothing of note. To my utter
disappointment, no sooner had I commenced the
ascent of the hill than rain began to fall. Hoping
it might pass off, I took shelter in a quarry with
fairly precipitous sides. A water-proof on one's arm
climbing a hill is an insupportable burden with
which I rarely encumbered myself. I remained here
for about an hour without any other sign of change
than that the heavy rain had become modified to a
persistent drizzle. As there was no hope of further
improvement, I made for Finstown, to wait for the
coach on its return. On my way I got *Lycopodium
alpinum*, which I had seen only once before ; and
down in the valley between Bigswell Hill and Germiston, in old peat-banks, I found *Carex muricata*
for the first time. Only once again did I meet
with it. Then amid the old quarries on the hill of
Heddle I got *Agrostis vulgaris*, var. *pumila*; so my
disappointment was not so keen as the earlier day
predicted.

A botanist in 'Orkney can rely on being treated
with kindness and consideration by the inhabitants.
The right to pass through any field or to explore even

c

the kailyard of a homestead in pursuit of his hobby
is seldom or never questioned. His presence in the
less accessible parts of the islands, seldom visited by
strangers, does give rise to much speculation at times
as to his object in wandering about in an aimless
fashion, but he is not interfered with. Though the
hobby does not bring one into close touch with
the people, it affords opportunities of meeting many
quaint characters in the more remote glens and
townships.

On one occasion Dr Flett and I, after climbing
the north side of the Ward, descended into the
valley of Rackwick, on the south side of the hill,
when a man approached us to enquire whether we
were looking for sheep to buy. We answered in
the negative. "Then you are excise-men," he said.
The sudden change of expression and the inquisitive
look told us plainly that he suspected us of belonging
to that once disliked class. "Can you give us a bit
of tobacco?" he next asked, with a rather suspicious
look, as much as to say, "There is no smuggled
tobacco in my possession, and you need not look
for any."

On another occasion, when visiting a farmer in
Harray, I said to his wife, "This burn looks pro-
mising. I mean to search its banks for a short
distance." She said, "Do you gather flo'ors?" "Yes,
I am deeply interested in that subject." "Are you?
In Harray we think nobody gathers flo'ors but
bairns and fules," she said. On another occasion a
worldly-wise old farmer said to me, "I see you're
gathering flo'ors like school-girls." "Yes," I said,

"God made the flowers for me and school-girls to admire, and through them to admire the super-abundant beauties of Nature. Some people seem to think God made nothing but shillings and pence." He was a man who kept the purse-strings pretty tight, and had little pleasure in anything beyond his savings.

On one of my earliest botanical excursions to Hoy, a friend and I went to Rackwick. The teacher there at that time was a young lady from Aberdeenshire. Having met her previously at the house of a mutual friend, we called. After chatting for a short time, she put the kettle on the fire, and said she would be absent for a few minutes, as she had to call on a neighbour. When she returned we were asked to guess her message. She told us. On the previous day, the unfortunate crofter had broken the family teapot, and as the grocer's shop was about four miles distant, she had borrowed that of our lady friend, who was in the plight of not being able to make tea for us till she got back her only teapot.

The botanist returns from his excursions at times flushed with success, bringing back with him new specimens, knowledge of new localities, new varieties, and new friendships formed. But there are other times when it is difficult for him to conceal his bitter disappointment. A plant has been reported from some locality not previously heard of. One is eager to procure specimens, and on the first opportunity sets off in search, only to find that the plant does not grow there—a mistake has been made by person can read his biography without seeing a man keen, observant, and possessed of a power of graphic description. In him we have a man with wonderful insight into the problems which he set himself to solve. Nothing of interest escaped his observation. His thorough botanical knowledge enabled him to gather plants from many almost inaccessible places seldom visited. Did he not visit the little island of Calf of Flotta to ascertain if *Oxalis acetosella* grew there ? Hoy, with its treasures, was a fruitful hunting ground for him. Finally, this man with such possibilities was stranded in Birsay, with, no doubt, a comfortable living, but amid work somewhat uncongenial. Witchcraft and superstition of the vilest type turned the sessions, of what should have been edifying intercourse, into police courts and criminal repertories which must have been hateful to a man of genius and nobility ; and then, to crown all, the nemesis of blindness pursued this man, from whose mind had flowed forth light and guidance amid the surrounding gloom ; and, finally, he was overwhelmed in utter darkness, but his mind, full of resources, sought interludes of relief in music, which somewhat solaced his last years. He died in his 49th year, full of disappointment from unfulfilled hopes.

ROBERT HEDDLE.

Robert Heddle was not only a botanist but an ornithologist of no mean order. He was joint-author of a " Natural History of Orkney," part i., with W. B. Baikie, M.D., of Kirkwall. It is rather difficult to arrive at the true estimate of a life's work done partly in this country and partly in Canada. He was uncle to the late John George Moodie-Heddle of Cletts, South Ronaldshay, who died a few years ago, and brother to Professor Mathew Forster Heddle, M.D., author of the " Mineralogy of Scotland," and Professor of Chemistry, St. Andrews University, both being sons of Robert Heddle of Melsetter and Hoy. He was, we believe, educated at the Edinburgh Academy, and studied for some time at Edinburgh University. One can readily understand how he spent the summer vacations in Walls and Hoy with the object of extending his knowledge of birds and plants. No one need wonder that these tastes were acquired early, when one has visited these lonely retreats so remote from the disturbing presence of man. Here one finds lochs dammed up amid the hills, fit homes for the shyer members of bird life. The moors are more extensive and the hills more numerous than one can realise from a passing view. The hills from the Melsetter side seem to rise in steps behind one another, and their bases interlace like some cunning network. Burns of all sizes—the homes of rare flowers—wind through the deep valleys to the sea. It is true that one's early environment often gives a youth's mind a bent which is pursued through life. What other pursuit could a lad, sensitive to the impress and charm of nature, dream of than to become a lover of flowers and birds; whilst his distinguished brother became one of the best authorities on geology and mineralogy. These were surely fitting spheres of labour for youths trained in the school of beetling cliffs and deep ravines, variegated meadows

Ronaldshay, and Papa Westray. This is a field
where a considerable amount of botanising remains
to be done. The lochs on the Mainland are better
supplied with boats, but even here a careful scrutiny
would probably result in the discovery of a few new
species.

In a county consisting of so many scattered
islands, the writing of a fairly accurate and com-
prehensive flora could hardly be the independent
work of one man. It is difficult at this time of
day to ascertain who were the first field botanists in
the county. There must have been some students
of Nature before Dr Wallace and the Rev. George
Low, but if such there were, their findings were no
doubt utilised by these men who have left us a
record of their botanical work. Succeeding these
we have Mr Robert Heddle, Dr Duguid, and Dr
Boswell, who were assisted in their work by other
lovers of the science, the best known of whom are
Dr Charles Clouston, of Sandwick, and Mr Robson,
schoolmaster, Birsay. In writing short, sketchy
biographies of the men who were the pioneers in
the study of systematic botany in this county, and
who are no longer with us, I feel that I am performing only a very pleasant duty in recording
their valuable and indispensable labours. It is not
easy to estimate the botanical value of Dr Barry's
work, who includes in his " History of Orkney" a
list of plants. Mr Patrick Neill and others tell us
that Dr Barry's list of Orkney plants is largely
an unacknowledged copy of the Rev. George Low's
work, and this seems very probable, as Dr Barry

does not in his history show that familiarity with plants which one would expect from the writer of a more or less correct flora of the county. Mr Patrick Neill says :—" While in Orkney in 1804, I had several opportunities of being in company with the late Dr Barry, the laborious author of the ' History of Orkney.' I was even favoured with a sight of the MS. of a ' Flora Orcadensis,' compiled by the Dr, partly from his own observations and partly (as he informed me) from MSS. left by the late Revd. Geo. Low, the northern assistant of Mr Pennant." Dr Joseph Anderson, in his introduction to Low's biography says, p. lxxiii. :—" Mr Low's ' Flora Orcadensis' is stated to have passed into the hands of the Revd. Dr George Barry, minister of Shapinsay, and to have been used by him in his ' History of Orkney,' published in 1800." Professor Traill says :—" I recollect the late Dr Barry shewing me a MS. flora, which he informed me was the work of Revd. Geo. Low."

GENERAL.

In preparing this hand-book of the Orkney flora, I have not attempted to write a description of each plant. That would have been superfluous, as anyone wishing to gain a familiar knowledge of the flora will find the information in standard botany books issued at a moderate price. My object has been to give as complete a list as possible of the local species and varieties, and of the places where they are to be found. I have, where possible, followed the 10th edition of the " London Catalogue"; but

as the description of plants—new varieties at least
—are not to be found there, but in inaccessible—to
me at least—botanical journals, I could not follow
it absolutely. I have to a greater extent laid the
" Manual of British Botany," 9th edition, by Professor
Babington, under contribution, and followed it more
closely than any other work. Sir J. D. Hooker's
" Student's Flora," 3rd edition ; Bentham and Hooker's
" Flora," 8th edition ; and Edmonston's 1st and 2nd
editions of the " Flora of Shetland" have been frequently referred to. Col. H. H. Johnston, D.Sc.,
C.B., F.L.S., published a valuable contribution in the
"Annals of Natural History of Scotland" in 1895,
from which a few species, especially of *Hieracia*,
have been taken, which form an interesting addition.
I have given the common names of plants, which
have been taken principally from the " Botanist's
Pocket Book." 6th edition, by W. R. Hayward, as
well as the scientific. The question has often been
asked me, " Why do you use scientific names, when
common, easily-remembered ones would suit as well ?"
Well, the difficulty is with the common names.
Many people use the same term for plants which
are quite different. Take " gowans," for example. I
have heard people apply the same term to three
different plants. Then " smerows" is the name
applied by some to *Lotus corniculatus*, by others
to *Trifolium repens*. Mr John Spence tells me that
in the Hillside, Birsay, it is applied to the latter ;
whilst in the neighbouring district of Beaquoy it
is used for the former. Common names, owing to
their indefinite application, had to be given up. I

at one time thought of incorporating in this "Flora" a list of the sea-weeds known to have been found round the coast of Orkney, and set to work to gather and name specimens. On second thoughts, however, I found that an additional list would be superfluous, as there is a thoroughly reliable book, "The Marine Algæ of the Orkney Islands," on the subject. It is a reprint from the "Proceedings of the Edinburgh Botanical Society," copies of which are now in the market at a moderate price. The author was the late Mr George W. Traill, Joppa, near Edinburgh. Mr Traill, as the name implies, was an Orcadian, being one of the Traills of North Ronaldshay, and a well-known authority on this subject. Besides this work, he also published "The Algæ of the Firth of Forth."

Half-a-dozen years ago it had never entered my mind that I should write a "Flora" of the county, although I had for nearly two decades previously taken a keen interest in the subject. The keenest botanist I have been associated with before his whole time was taken up with his own work as geologist, was John S. Flett, D.Sc., LL.D., F.R.S., Chief of the Geological Survey, Scotland. I once expressed my regret that he had not published a "Flora" of the county before he had received an important appointment in geology. He replied to say that in the event of my undertaking this work he would call on Mr Arthur Bennett, F.L.S., Croydon, London, one of the greatest living authorities on systematic botany, and ask him to examine any doubtful or rare specimens I cared to send him. 1

took his advice, with the result that my herbarium
is now fully representative of the flora of the county.
I have visited all the larger islands, and as a rule
spent a few days in each. Flotta is the largest I
have not been able to visit. Mr Arthur Bennett,
F.L.S., is deeply interested in the flora of the North
of Scotland, and examined the specimens sent him
with great care. The notes added to the more
variable species testify to this.

When help was so accessible, and many eager
workers in the field, my only compunction is that
the publication of this work has been proceeded
with too early. It would certainly have been freer
from errors and fuller had the time of preparation
been prolonged ; but there is on the other hand this
compensation, that my botanical friends in this
research work will have a hand-book with which
to compare notes. As time goes on additions will
be made and errors eradicated, so that finally we
shall be enabled to claim for the "Flora" a close
approach to accuracy. My only plea for lenient
criticism from fellow-botanists is that the time for
this responsible task was snatched from a very busy
professional life, and that in my pursuit of botanical
knowledge I have had to visit a large number of
widely-scattered parishes and islands, which, in the
absence of a regular service of any kind, are made
more inaccessible than most other parts of the British
Isles. A botanist from the centre of England once
put it thus, "You live in a county where, if you
desire to reach a place ten or twelve miles distant
as the crow flies, you have to take probably two

days to reach it, and even then only when available communication is possible." These difficulties were aggravated by the fact that my holidays commenced with the time of harvest, which is considered early when it takes place at the beginning of September; but then an early harvest means an early floral season, so that the compensation was nil.

BIOGRAPHICAL.

Dr Wallace.

The earliest list extant of Orkney plants was drawn up by James Wallace, M.D., F.R.S., in his "Account of the Orkney Islands," published in 1700. This was a reprint of the work, with additions, which was written by his father and published in 1693. His father was the Rev. James Wallace, minister of the Cathedral Church, Kirkwall, who died of fever in 1688 at the early age of fifty years. Dr Wallace prefaces his list with these notes :—" I did not find this country so well stored with plants as I expected. I found none of the *Malva* kind, nor several other plants that I thought might have agreed well enough with this country ; but such as I did find, I thought an account of them might not be unacceptable, though I am far from pretending this to be so very exact as it should have been ; these being the names of those only I have by me." The list of plants did not appear in the 1st, the father's, edition. In Dr Wallace's edition of 1700, the list occupies a prominent place in chapter ii. From the introductory remarks quoted above, it is

more than likely that Dr Wallace was the botanist
having a herbarium of Orkney plants beside him.
He mentions the order of *Malvaceæ* as having no
representative in the county. This is still almost
true. I never saw one growing in the open country;
but about a month ago some pupils brought very
fine specimens of *Malva moschata* from a grass field
on the farm of Greentofts. They had come with
seeds, no doubt, and the lovely summer enabled
them to develop and flower beautifully. This is an
exceedingly interesting list, containing some 260
species, at so early a date. Subsequent botanists
must have had their work greatly simplified by
having so complete a " Flora" to work from. A few
of these were garden plants; several of them are
not now found in Orkney, and it is even doubtful
whether some of them ever grew here. I may give
a few extinct or mistaken ones culled from his list :—
Adiantum aureum, golden maidenhair; *Hypericum
androsæmum*, St. John's wort ; *Campanula rotundifolia*, hair-bell ; *Carduus nutans*, musk thistle ;
Cynoglossum officinale, hound's-tongue ; *Gentianella
autumnalis*, dwarf gentian ; *Geranium Columbium*,
dove's foot; *Hypericum quadranglum*, St. Peter's
wort; *Sium minimum*, least water-parsnip. His list
is rather curious; several of his species must have been
non-indigenous. His dwarf gentian may probably
have been the plant I found in North Ronaldshay
and Swanney, Firsay, and now named *Gentiana
Baltica*. There is much interest attached to a list
published a few years before Linnæus was born, when
classification and nomenclature were in their infancy.

Rev. George Low.

The Rev. George Low, minister of Birsay, a native of Edzell, in Forfarshire, was tutor in the family of Mr Robert Graham of Stromness from 1771-1773. He was licensed by the Presbytery of Cairston in 1771, after having completed his divinity course at St. Andrews. Round Breckness, for long the home of Graham, Low had excellent facilities for studying natural history, which we find he did most assiduously. By the help of microscopes, one of which, a water one, he is said to have constructed, he did a considerable amount of interesting microscopic work which was never published. One can readily understand from a cursory glance at his " Tour through Orkney and Shetland in 1774 " that he was a thorough and well-informed field botanist. He is every now and again dropping on rare plants, and taking special note thereof. It is unfortunate that Dr Barry did not acknowledge his indebtedness to Mr Low. It was when tutor in Mr Graham's family that Mr Pennant, the celebrated naturalist and antiquary, encouraged him to make the famous " Tour through Orkney and Zetland." This " Tour" was not published till 1879. He was also author of " Fauna Orcadensis," published in 1813. He married Miss Helen Tyrie, only daughter of the parish minister of Stromness. Low was a wonderful man ; he had all the scientific enthusiasm and methodical system of Hooker or White of Selborne, but living as he did far from the centre of scientific thought, many insuperable difficulties arose that prevented his works from receiving the recognition they deserved. No person can read his biography without seeing a man keen, observant, and possessed of a power of graphic description. In him we have a man with wonderful insight into the problems which he set himself to solve. Nothing of interest escaped his observation. His thorough botanical knowledge enabled him to gather plants from many almost inaccessible places seldom visited. Did he not visit the little island of Calf of Flotta to ascertain if *Oxalis acetosella* grew there ? Hoy, with its treasures, was a fruitful hunting ground for him. Finally, this man with such possibilities was stranded in Birsay, with, no doubt, a comfortable living, but amid work somewhat uncongenial. Witchcraft and superstition of the vilest type turned the sessions, of what should have been edifying intercourse, into police courts and criminal repertories which must have been hateful to a man of genius and nobility ; and then, to crown all, the nemesis of blindness pursued this man, from whose mind had flowed forth light and guidance amid the surrounding gloom ; and, finally, he was overwhelmed in utter darkness, but his mind, full of resources, sought interludes of relief in music, which somewhat solaced his last years. He died in his 49th year, full of disappointment from unfulfilled hopes.

ROBERT HEDDLE.

Robert Heddle was not only a botanist but an ornithologist of no mean order. He was joint-author of a " Natural History of Orkney," part i., with W. B. Baikie, M.D., of Kirkwall. It is rather difficult to arrive at the true estimate of a life's work done partly in this country and partly in Canada. He was uncle to the late John George Moodie-Heddle of Cletts, South Ronaldshay, who died a few years ago, and brother to Professor Mathew Forster Heddle, M.D., author of the "Mineralogy of Scotland," and Professor of Chemistry, St. Andrews University, both being sons of Robert Heddle of Melsetter and Hoy. He was, we believe, educated at the Edinburgh Academy, and studied for some time at Edinburgh University. One can readily understand how he spent the summer vacations in Walls and Hoy with the object of extending his knowledge of birds and plants. No one need wonder that these tastes were acquired early, when one has visited these lonely retreats so remote from the disturbing presence of man. Here one finds lochs dammed up amid the hills, fit homes for the shyer members of bird life. The moors are more extensive and the hills more numerous than one can realise from a passing view. The hills from the Melsetter side seem to rise in steps behind one another, and their bases interlace like some cunning network. Burns of all sizes—the homes of rare flowers—wind through the deep valleys to the sea. It is true that one's early environment often gives a youth's mind a bent which is pursued through life. What other pursuit could a lad, sensitive to the impress and charm of nature, dream of than to become a lover of flowers and birds; whilst his distinguished brother became one of the best authorities on geology and mineralogy. These were surely fitting spheres of labour for youths trained in the school of beetling cliffs and deep ravines, variegated meadows and winding burns, and rocky escarpments with sheltered crevices for rare ferns and rarer flowers. With such a training—at one time storing up knowledge in the seats of learning, at another classifying and identifying birds and plants—one is surely well qualified for life's battle. His first occupation was, I believe, that of farmer in Hobbister, Orphir, of which his father was proprietor. He grew tired of sheep-farming and stock-rearing, as was to be expected, and having secured a situation in the Bank of Montreal, Toronto, he lived there with his wife, a daughter of Dr Duguid, Kirkwall. He and his father-in-law were joint authors of a MS. " Flora Orcadensis," which was never published. His letters written to his niece, Miss Mary Heddle, now Mrs Moodie, London, show the bias of his mental activities. Here are a few quotations : — " But then imagine the delight of getting away in the evening into the deep, deep wood, where sunlight scarcely enters and where the tall pines cling together overhead, and wandering underneath we find strange flowers too numerous and varied. Indeed, they come up so fast, blossom so short, and vanish so speedily, that a botanist tied by the heels all day, and only escaping for a hurried evening scramble, feels many a sad regret at not being able to keep up with their exuberance, and bewails species seen but in bud, a week afterwards in seed, whilst its gay blossoms never gladdened his sight. Still I have culled and rudely pressed many kinds, to me a joy and solace such as my bank-fellows know nothing of." Again : " I tumble in to dinner about 6 p.m. inclined for nought but wandering afield. I bring home occasionally huge bundles of plants, and, sad to say, have only time to press a few of them ; still, what a luxury to a lover of such." These quotations show that here is a keen observer of Nature, a man with an insatiable love of flowers occupying every spare moment in pursuit of his hobbies, until at last the strain of confinement, intensified perhaps by uncongenial occupation, saps the health, and the need is felt for change and rest. Mr Heddle returned to his native heaths and sea-girt islands, hoping their bracing airs would restore his health, but all in vain. He died in Kirkwall on 28th August 1860, at the early age of 33 years, and was buried in St Magnus Churchyard. He left a widow and one son. Mrs Heddle subsequently married Mr John Bruce, Sheriff-Clerk, Kirkwall. This biographical sketch of the life of Mr Robert Heddle is the story of one who was not permitted to outlive the day's labour, but fell tired and wounded on the battlefield. There was for him no time of pleasant retirement to look back on the strivings of youth, the struggles and victories and defeats of maturity, to count up the gains and losses and reject the wrong and confirm the right. In the full tide of his career, in the full tide of his intellectual strength, with more apparently in front of him than behind him, he was laid low.

ALEXANDER RUSSELL DUGUID, M.D.

Dr Duguid was born at Borrowstounness, or Bo'ness, Linlithgowshire, in the year 1798, and was the youngest son of the family. Shortly after his birth his father, the Rev. John Duguid, was presented

d

by the patron to the parish of Evie and Rendall. Dr Duguid there spent his early life, amid the quiet and retirement of a country parish, but surrounded by the natural beauties of land and sea, which often develop those tendencies inherent in us from ancestors whose mode of life engendered them. Face to face with the varied phenomena of land and shore, with swirling eddies and wave-washed cliffs, with a flora and fauna of great beauty and variety, he became a zealous student of Nature. It is said he early formed a kindly and benevolent spirit, which was remarkably developed in after life. After studying three years at Aberdeen, he entered the University of Edinburgh with the view of studying medicine. In 1819 he graduated, and immediately thereafter commenced the practice of his profession in Kirkwall. He is said to have introduced " a scale of fees very different from what people had been accustomed to. With Dr Duguid, money-making was not a passion. His heart was in his work, and his desire was to do good to others." He was an enthusiastic student of natural history, and devoted a considerable portion of his leisure to this department of scientific research. There was not a spot in the island where a rare plant was to be found with which he was not familiar. In 1831 he was married to Elizabth Ann, daughter of Capt. Thomas M'Kenzie of Groundwater, Orphir, by whom he had three sons and four daughters. His wife predeceased him in 1845. On the completion of the fiftieth year of his professional life in Kirkwall he was publicly presented with a silver claret jug and a purse of sovereigns. The jug bore the following inscription:—" Presented to Alexander Russell Duguid, Esq., M.D., L.R.C.S.E., on the occasion of his completing 50 years' practice as a physician in Kirkwall, by his friends and acquaintances, and the community in general, as a mark of the respect and esteem in which he is held for his long and able services."

Dr Boswell

As I do not wish to do any injustice, from lack of the requisite knowledge, to such an honoured name as that of Dr Boswell, I shall take the liberty of copying an excellent monograph to the distinguished botanist and entomologist as it appeared in the " Scottish Naturalist," vol. ix., p. 243:—" We record with regret the death, on 31st Jan. 1888, of Dr John Thomas Irvine Boswell Boswell of Balmuto, Fifeshire, perhaps better known as Dr J. T. Boswell Syme. He was the son of the late Mr Patrick Syme, of Edinburgh and Dollar, who married Miss Boswell, a daughter of Lord Balmuto, a Lord of Session, and for many years Sheriff of Fife. Dr Boswell was born in Edinburgh in 1822, and educated at Dollar Academy and Edinburgh University. He qualified as a civil engineer, and while engaged in surveys on the west coast of Scotland he occupied his leisure time in dredging and botanising. After a few years he gave up the profession of civil engineer and turned his attention entirely to the study of natural history, a science for which he had shown a remarkable aptitude from childhood. In 1849 he visited his brother-in-law, Mr Fortescue of Swanbister, Orphir, where he made a collection of

birds and studied the plants, moths, and beetles of
the district, besides devoting much of his time to
dredging. He continued during the rest of his life
to take an enthusiastic interest in the flora and
entomology of the Orkney Islands (especially the
Hieraceæ and *Naiadaceæ*), where he found one or
two plants new to Britain and several varieties
differing from the typical. From 1851 to 1868 Dr
Boswell (then Mr Syme) lived in London, where he
held the position of Curator to the Botanical Society
of London, and Lecturer on Botany to the Charing
Cross and Middlesex School of Medicine. He also
lectured on Natural Science at the New College,
Edinburgh, for a year previous to the appointment
of Dr Duns. On 28th April 1856, he married Miss
Hardwick, daughter of the late Mr Hardwick,
solicitor, London. In April 1868 Dr Boswell left
London and came to reside at Balmuto, Fife, where
he spent the remainder of his life. In 1875 he
succeeded to this property, and assumed the name of
Boswell, under the will of his uncle, Mr Boswell of
Balmuto and Kingcausie. Dr Boswell was a keen
lepidopterist and coleopterist; but his interest was
chiefly centred in the botany of the North Temperate
Zone. The chief work of his life was editing the 3rd
edition of 'Sowerby's English Botany.' He entirely
re-wrote the scientific portion of this standard work
on British plants, which extends to twelve volumes.
He describes the plants from his own observations,
and it is in these descriptions that his genius is most
apparent. In all his work he was ably assisted by
his wife, who acted as his amanuensis. In recognition

of his great scientific attainments, the University of St. Andrews conferred upon him the degree of LL.D. He was besides a Fellow of the Linnæan Society, and of the Royal Botanical Society of Edinburgh, and a member of the Ray Society. Dr Boswell was the most eminent authority of the day on critical and doubtful British plants, and such plants, together with new discoveries, were constantly submitted to him for classification. He formed a most valuable herbarium of British and European species, and also made a valuable entomological collection. In the garden of Balmuto he had a fine collection of bulbs, irises, and helibores, besides a number of other interesting British and foreign plants. For the last few years of his life he was debarred by failing health from active work, but up to the last his interest in scientific matters never flagged. He was naturally of an unassuming disposition; only those who knew him personally understood the extent of his researches, the soundness of his conclusions, and the value of his opinions on almost every subject. . . The loss to the scientific world, as well as to his friends, can hardly be over-estimated. He leaves a widow, a daughter, and two sons, the elder of whom is now representative of the old family of Boswells of Balmuto, and is preparing for the Scottish Bar."

MR PATRICK NEILL.

Just about one hundred years after the publications of the Wallaces—father and son—on Orkney, we get a deeply interesting account of these islands, especially their flora, from the pen of Patrick Neill,

M.A., secretary to the Natural History Society of Edinburgh, in the year 1806. This book is called "A Tour through some of the Islands of Orkney and Zetland, with a View chiefly to Objects of Natural History." He added about 100 phanerogams and ferns and 50 mosses to the list previously published in Dr Barry's history—Low's collection, as already stated. Low's list enumerated 312 species, but Mr Neill says some half-a-dozen at least were spurious. This raises the list of native species to 462. A great deal of interest attaches to this "Tour," because Neill was a thoroughly qualified field botanist, and took special note of all he saw. He visited the best botanical fields in these islands—Hoy, Walls, and Rousay. His "Tour" is very suggestive, for he not only records his observations, but he expresses valuable opinions on subjects relating to natural history, economics, estate management, and sociology. He makes suggestions as to the betterment of the people, especially Shetlanders, who seem at that time to have been the victims of a vicious system of truck, which has since been reduced to a minimum under the enlightened supervision of the Crofters' and other Commissions. His knowledge of birds and bird-life was almost as complete as that of flowers. Orkney must then have been an *incognita terra* to botanists. Just think of the possibility of adding 156 new species to the flora in one summer. Most of his discoveries have been confirmed by later botanists. One of the most interesting was *Hypericum elodes*, which he records as growing on the side of the Burn of Berriedale. I am not sure that it has ever been

found since—certainly not of late. He is so specific
that no doubt can be entertained as to its existence
there a hundred years ago. He says that in a little
loch on Knitchen Hill, Rousay, there was a plant
like a *sparganium*, but not in flower. Its leaves
were more like *Poa fluitans*, with floating leaves.
It differed from *sparganium* in having narrower,
coarser, and longer leaves. This description agrees
very well with the *sparganium* growing in a small
loch along the road from Hoy to Rackwick, which
is now designated by the name *Sparganium affine*,
var. *microcephalum*. The Rev. A. Marshall discovered it in 1910. Some day *Hypericum elodes*
will turn up, to the delight of Orcadian botanists.

Dr. Clouston.

The next extension of the list of plants indigenous
to Orkney was made by Charles Clouston, LL.D., one
of the most active of naturalists and one who did
more for the advancement of his own generation in
Orkney in a knowledge of Science than any other
Orcadian. He was a son of the parish minister of
Stromness; was born in 1800, ordained in 1826,
became minister of Sandwick in 1832, and died in
1885, after a lifetime full of good and profitable work
—an example to all who have spare time to devote to
projects of utility. He was minister of a large parish,
medical adviser to most of his parishioners, for he was
an L.C.S.E. and meteorologist for the long period of
58 years, but still he found time to devote to the
study of botany, geology, and local antiquities. In
addition to these varied activities, he was the guiding

spirit in the founding of the Natural History Society
of Stromness, in the management of which he took an
exceedingly active part ; he was president from 1837
to 1885. It was during his presidency that the
museum was commenced, and to it he devoted much
time and energy. To the archæological and geological
sections of the museum he presented many specimens.
To-day the collection as a whole is a credit to
Stromness—being kept clean and bright, and the
arrangement of the exhibits being systematic and
easily intelligible. We hope it will some day have a
full herbarium of Orkney plants, as the museum of
Thurso has of Caithness plants. Dr. Clouston's additions to the published lists of Low and Neill were
recorded in his able and interesting account of the
Orkney Isles in " Anderson's Guide to the Highlands
and Islands of Scotland," which, to this day, is interesting and accurate. In his plant list there are two
or three of special interest :—*Senecio viscosus* was
reported by him to have grown in Harray and Firth.
This species has not been found recently. He was the
first, I understand, to add *Chara aspera* to the list of
British plants. In his list are also *Draba hirta* and
Primula elator, which have not been found for some
time as far as I know. His special study, however,
was marine algæ. During his day the study of the
marine algæ round Orkney was actively pursued also
by Dr. Pollexfen, Mr James Cursiter, F.S.A.Scot., Mrs
Moffat, and her sister, Miss Watt, Skail. Dr Clouston's
name will long be held in reverence in Orkney, and
especially in Sandwick and Stromness, for his self-
sacrificing devotion to his parochial duties as well

as to the advancement of scientific knowledge in Orkney.

DR FORTESCUE.

By far the most complete list of Orkney plants previously published was edited by Dr Fortescue of Swanbister, Orphir, and Kingcaussie, Aberdeen, and published in the " Scottish Naturalist," vol. vi., 1881-82, edited by F. B. White, M.D,, F.L.S.; and vol. i., new series, 1883-84, edited by J. W. H. Traill, A.M., M.D., F.L.S., F.R.S., Professor of Botany in the University of Aberdeen. Dr Fortescue was then a farmer in the farm of Swanbister, which belonged at that time to his father, and now belongs to himself. Whether his love of natural history in its twofold aspect—plant and bird life—had anything to do with his desire to follow this pursuit, I know not, but it is no more than a truism to say that his life as an agriculturist was made both more interesting and complete from the fact that his spare time was devoted to a pursuit so congenial to his tastes, and a healthy reaction to the petty irritations common to the life of an agriculturist. His training for becoming a student of botany was of the very best, His uncle, Dr Boswell, on a few occasions, spent his holidays in Orkney, with his headquarters at Swanbister. Under his efficient tuition and guidance—for he was a reliable and accurate specialist, and one of the best masters of the science of botany which last century produced—his pupil was exceptionally fortunate. Dr Fortescue, too, showed by his careful and original work that he had either inherited or acquired the same indispensable qualities.

He lived in one of the best centres in Orkney from the point of view of the field botanist. Behind Swanbister lay the extensive range of the Orphir and Stenness hills, and in front, across a narrow arm of the sea, lay Hoy and Walls, by far the best botanical hunting ground in Orkney. The material on which his work was based was the plant list in MS. form compiled by Dr Duguid and Mr Heddle, which the latter was preparing, no doubt, for part ii. of his "Natural History of Orkney." As Dr Fortescue is still in his prime and as great an enthusiast as ever, with only the earlier stages of his life's work behind him, there is no need of saying more here. He is now equipped, as never before, with the modern culture and learning of a university whose professor in this branch of science is an ardent expert. Let us hope Dr Fortescue may yet have time to return to his first love of Orcadian botany. Had he not left the county and engaged in professional work in Aberdeen, I would not have undertaken a work rightly belonging to him. His list, however, was a sealed book to most of those attracted by this hobby. Some handbook of the subject was urgently needed. I have already said that I felt it my duty to respond to frequent requests to prepare this "Flora." When Dr Fortescue learned of the undertaking, he very generously and kindly got part ii. of his list, which could not be obtained in the book market, typewritten, and by adding notes of his experience and knowledge since his list appeared, rendered my obligations to him very deep indeed. His readiness to assist, and his willingness to give of labour ungrudgingly, are well-known characteristics of his.

ACKNOWLEDGMENTS.

Dr GRANT is a most enthusiastic botanist. The professional duties of a doctor in Orkney, we all know, are very arduous, and it says much for him that amid them all he found pleasure in occupying his spare moments in making himself thoroughly acquainted with the flora of the Mainland and the South Isles, traversed by him in his professional rounds. He has undertaken, too, the laborious task of compiling the moss section of the cryptogamic flora of the same district, and has made a noteworthy collection of over 250 mosses. This is all the more creditable when we reflect that this was a neglected field, and had only previously been dealt with in a very superficial way. His work is a valuable contribution to this "Flora," and renders it much more complete than otherwise it would have been. If any part of botanical work requires patience and expert knowledge it is this. My indebtedness to him in other respects is great. There are at least three plants which, but for him, would not have been included in the present list. These are :— *Potamogeton pusillus*, var. *Berchtoldi ; Ranunculus sceleratus*, and *Cornus suecica.* For specimens of these and much valuable help otherwise, I beg to express my indebtedness.

To Professor JAMES W. H. TRAIL, M.A., M.D., F.R.S., F.L.S., my best thanks are due. His kindness in offering assistance and his readiness to help are pleasant remembrances. More especially is this the case when one knows how exacting are the duties

of the Professors of Botany in our Universities.
Not only did he comply heartily with any request
I made on his time, but he enlisted the sympathy
of one or two who he thought would be of service
to me.

I also gratefully acknowledge my indebtedness
to Mr GEORGE SCARTH, M.A., who was for some
years assistant to Professor Balfour, Edinburgh University. He has examined the flora of the West
Mainland and the neighbourhood of Kirkwall pretty
thoroughly. He was the first to find *Carex limosa*
in Orkney, on the moor between Hillside, Birsay,
and Evie. He has already made a valuable contribution to the flora of Orkney in his "Ecology of
Orkney Vegetation in its Relation to the Different
Classes of Soil." The paper was published in the
"Proceedings of the Edinburgh Botanical Society"
for 1911, and is full of interest and suggestion. He
and I spent a very profitable week in Sanday and
Papa Westray in September 1909, and were rewarded
by finding the following rare plants :—*Thalictrum
minus*, var. *dunense*, and *Sium angustifolium* in
Sanday ; and *Ranunculus hederacea* and *Linum
catharticum*, var. *condensatium*, in Papa Westray.
We also got at that time large numbers of *Primula
scotica*, var. *nova*, in sandy links of Papa Westray.

Col. H. H. JOHNSTON, D.Sc., M.D., C.B., F.L.S.,
has been an unwearied student of Orcadian botany.
During his several intermittent periods of furlough
from his medical duties in India, Africa, Egypt,

Gibraltar, and elsewhere, he has never lost his keen interest in the flora of his native county. From Dr Fortescue's list one can see that the Colonel was a recognised authority on Orkney plants many years ago. *Utricularia minor* was one of his earliest discoveries. There are several *Hieracia, Ranunculaceæ,* and other rare plants justly credited to his name. He has recently greatly increased my obligations to him by sending me lists of all his latest "finds." Some of these, I regret, have come too late to find their proper place under their various orders; so that we have to be satisfied with adding them as an appendix.

JOHN S. FLETT, D.Sc., LL.D., F.R.S., Director of the Geological Survey of Scotland, has given me valuable help in addition to what I have already acknowledged. He has written a very able and interesting paper for this "Flora" on the geological structure of the islands, and the re-introduction of their flora after their entire denudation by the ice sheets of the Great Ice Age, and subsequent changes. All botanists and geologists who read this paper will, I feel sure, be grateful to him for expressing in clear and simple language his interpretations of an intricate and difficult subject, and making it readable and intelligible.

Mr WILLIAM McKAY, J.P., F.E.I.S., and Mr JOHN FIRTH, Finstown, drew up a very interesting list of plants which were at one time used medicinally in Orkney. This list, with the additions sent by Mr

JOHN SPENCE, Overabist, Hillside, Birsay, forms a valuable contribution to this flora. It is curious that the lists from Firth and Birsay, and the uses to which plants were put, were almost identical. These old, time-honoured customs in our islands give us a glimpse of the way by which the skill of the medical practitioner was usurped by quackery, and the best religious influences and the most inspiring teachings were often nullified by the grossest super-stitions. Every disease was supposed to have an antidote—a sure remedy—in some plant or plants which only the quack knew or thought he knew. These applications of plant cures were often accom-panied by incantations and bewitchery of a type which showed that the intelligence of the people was at a low ebb. No doubt there was an undercurrent of truth in these remedies, for their medical saws, like their weather saws, were gained by experience and observation. To both my best thanks are due. Mr McKay sent me several rare plants in addition, and otherwise gave me valuable assistance.

In addition to the above, I wish also to express my indebtedness to Mr and Mrs SCOTT, Stenness; to Mr and Mrs INKSTER, Holm; to Mr OMOND, Kir-buster, Orphir; and Mr JOHN SPENCE, Overabist, Hillside, Birsay, for keeping me informed of rare plants found in their respective localities. My daughter, Mrs CLOUSTON, M.A., and her husband, Mr DAVID CLOUSTON, M.A., B.Sc. of the Agricultural Department, India, revised many of the proofs during a holiday at home, for which I beg to thank them.

SUBJECTS CO-RELATED TO THE BOTANY OF ORKNEY.

CLIMATIC FACTORS.

THE climate of Orkney is insular, and free from the extremes, not only of continental areas, but of the inland districts of large islands, as of Great Britain. Temperature seldom falls very low, and as seldom rises high. One of the chief obstacles to plant growth is the unseasonable Springs. Winter is often prolonged to the end of March, and sometimes to the middle of April. The first three months are the coldest. July and August are the warmest; they are also the best for botanical excursions. There is another factor, which causes even more destruction to plant life, and that is the sudden changes from mild to severe within the space of two or three days. March is proverbially severe and trying on plant life. Some fine week—for it has its periods of mildness and sunshine, and Nature responds to the call—when trees are budding and the growth of plants sends their sap in circulation; this early promise may be in the iron grip of frost before a dozen hours have passed. This is, I believe, why so many orders and families of flowers are not represented in our floral treasures. The orders of *Malvaceæ* and *Nymphaceæ* and the families of *Arabis* and *Campanula* are not represented by a single plant; whilst the larger families of *Hypericum* and *Centaurea* have only one each. These are only a few of the unrepresented families and orders.

Meteorological observations have been made in the county for the long period of eighty-seven years. During this time the lowest temperature was 8°, which occurred on 18th January 1881. The highest was 76°, on the 16th July 1876. It is the temperature range for the same month rather than the absolute extremes that test the enduring power of plants. During this year, 1913, January had a minimum temperature of 31°, and a maximum of 48°, showing a range of 17°. February had a range of 15°. The mean difference for March between day and night temperatures is only 8°, whilst at Nairn it is 13°. During April it is 9° in Orkney and 15° at Nairn. When snow falls during the earlier months, it generally acts as a protective covering for plants; but in March and April the sun's rays clear off the snow and leave the plants exposed to the killing influence of "black frost." In 1906, the absolute temperature range for March was 30°, but this is exceptional, for it seldom exceeds 20°. 1895 was a year of great severity. The temperature ranges were—January, 20°; February, 22°; March, 26°; and April, 30°; but snow fell, or covered the ground, for 24 days in January, 24 in February, 4 in March, and 5 in April.

In April of that year, on the 4th, the temperature fell to 25·6°, and next day it rose to 45·6°—a range of 20° in two days. Next to sudden changes of temperature, high winds affect vegetable growth. Fortunately our strong gales occur during the winter months, and the more moderate during the other seasons. Vegetation on exposed hill-sides and on low-lying islands is of stunted growth. *Caluna, Empetrum,* and other plants show in some cases lines of exposed stems and roots where the wind has not only withered the plants but carried off some of the soil from the roots. These things are seen on the west and south-west hill-sides. A gale is reckoned by the Meteorological Office as having a velocity of 40 miles or upwards, and these are frequent.

MEANS OF OBSERVATIONS IN ORKNEY
For 33 Years—1873-1905.

Rainy days.	Snowy days.	Days on which hail fell.	Thunder storms.	Clear sky.	Overcast.	Gales.
219	31	14	6	31	156	79

The mean annual rainfall is 37 inches, and the mean annual sunshine is 1185 hours, which compares favourably with Edinburgh—1164 hours. Winter gales reached their maximum in November 1893, with a velocity of 96 miles. The summer maximum occurred in June 1890, with a maximum velocity of 75 miles. This dreadful gale caused vegetation everywhere, but especially cereals, to put on a yellowish, withered appearance, as if the crops were partially destroyed; but the grain was not in ear, and the broad leaves alone suffered. In a few weeks the earth was once more clothed in a mantle of green.

e

Nowhere have I seen plants stunted as in North Ronaldshay. On the tops of the higher hills it is also well defined. *Geum rivale* is a tall plant of 1½ or 2 feet. One had somehow strayed half-way up the Ward Hill, Hoy, and was dwarfed and creeping. St. John's wort, *Lotus corniculatus*, and others are met with on exposed surfaces, and look as if they were creeping plants.

We need say little about rainfall, as it is seldom plants suffer from want of moisture. The annual rainfall is not excessive—37 inches—and is low compared with the west of Scotland and some of its higher regions. The supply of moisture, especially in summer, depends more on the manner of precipitation than the quantity. Drizzly rains, as we frequently have, and fogs, keep vegetation well supplied with this *sine qua non* of plant life.

PEAT BOGS.

Peat is a heterogeneous mass of dead plants. The layers are composed of the remains of different plants which for the time being were dominant. They accumulated under varying conditions which prevailed over long periods of time back to the Great Ice Age. The deeper peat bogs, found generally in valleys, were formed where marsh conditions prevailed. The plants which constituted the formation were chiefly monocotyledons—aquatic plants, sedges and grasses. A little mud accumulated with these, and on the soil so formed plants characteristic of the bog grew—*e.g.*, cotton grass, sphagnum, carices, rushes, &c. So the process of accumulation goes on, whilst decomposition proceeds apace under the action of bacteria, fungi, and the smaller animals. This decomposition differs from decay on exposed lands, owing to the water-logged soil shutting out the atmosphere, and humic and organic acids are formed, which act as preservatives. The White Moss between St. Andrews and Holm is one of the best examples of a boggy peat moss in Orkney. The surface is too wet for *Caluna vulgaris* to grow with any vigour. It is there in abundance, but conditions are unfavourable for its successful growth, owing to the sodden nature of the soil. The surface consists mainly of slightly rounded, hummocky braes, with low interspaces, where sphagnum grows in abundance. These sphagna are always soaking with water, as, owing to the flat surface, there is no drainage. The sphagnum is like a sponge—it not only retains the water for a long time against drought, but it extracts moisture from the dew and mist present during fog and dewfall. It is rather curious to find *Drosera*—both *rotundofolia* and *Anglica*—in great abundance in the water-logged depressions among the sphagnum.

ECOLOGY.

Quite a new branch of botanical science has been introduced in the last decade, viz., the study of plant associations. Ecology bears the same relation to botany that sociology does to humanity. Both are comparatively new subjects, and are now receiving much attention and study. In a general way the communities that plants form have been known for long, but a detailed study of the relation of such groups of plants has not been made till quite recently. We find groups of quite dissimilar plants forming communities according to the nature of the soil. There are heathy, marshy, and sea-shore communities, as well as those of sand-dunes and salt-marshes. Take as an example the sand-dunes. Most of the plants are binders : *Psamma arenaria, Carex arenaria, Triticum junceum,* and *Triticum repens.* There is a large area of land in Orkney which has not yet been cultivated, so that there is ample room for associations of plants. In many little lochs plant communities are gradually filling them up, and ultimately swampy meadow-land will have been formed. No better illustration of this can be seen than the platforms of bullrush and *Phalaris arundacea* formed in some lochs. These plants with stiff stems catch the drift of the lochs—weeds and broken reeds— until several lochs have spaces like huge platforms formed out into the water, often in a crescent shape, at the edge of which bullrushes and stiff grasses push out, farther and farther, year by year, until there is left this fertile land which bears the local name of the "reeds." These recovered areas can be seen in most of our smaller lochs, as in Isbister, Banks, and Sabiston Lochs, Birsay ; Græmeshall Loch, Holm ; Bea, Sanday ; Milldam, Westray ; and Wasdale, Firth A few years ago, a strong easterly gale, with high tide, laid bare several yards of soil beneath a sand-bank in Newark Bay. A whole net-work of interwoven roots of sand-binders, closely matted, showed how perfectly these perform the task of sand-binding.

ISLAND FLORAS.

It is very noticeable that when an island is separated from the mainland by shallow channels, even though comparatively wide, the island flora corresponds very closely to that of the mainland. The flora of the British Isles differs very slightly from that of the continent opposite it. We may conclude that islands separated by shallow seas have been isolated for a much shorter time than those separated by deep channels. Great Britain has the "silver streak" we call the German Ocean, no part of which is as deep as Loch Lomond. We find, on the other hand, that the Azores, Madeira, and the Canary Islands, with a depth of many feet separating them from the coasts of Portugal and Morocco, have floras distinct from the nearest lands ; and have flowers, the lineal descendants of late geological times, mixed with a few strays and waifs from the continent. Then Madagascar is separated from Africa by a broad and deep channel, and has a flora differing much from the part of the continent of Africa opposite to it.

The flora of Orkney corresponds so closely to that of Caithness on the one hand, and of Shetland on the other, that as the floras of the three counties come to be better known, their differences are disappearing, e.g., Ruppia rostellata, var. nana, when first discovered in the Oyce of Firth by Dr Boswell, was new to Great Britain ; now it has been found along the sea border of Sutherland and Ross. Elevation and nature of subsoil, depending on the rock formation underneath, do constitute conditions which determine slight changes. The serpentine rocks of Unst have *Arenaria Norvegica,* which is found nowhere else. The Ward Hill of Hoy possesses one species not found in the other two— Caithness and Shetland—viz., *Dryas octopetala.* Of the 560 odd species found in Orkney—rather more in Caithness and less in Shetland—there are comparatively few species found in one county and not in the others, or in two counties and not in the third. I am not using the term " three counties" politically, but botanically.

This is a list of plants not common to the three counties, prepared by Mr Arthur Bennett, F.L.S., and published in "Annals of Scottish Natural History," January 1909 :—

NAME OF PLANT.	Orkney.	Caithness.	Shetland.
Arabis petræa	No ...	No ...	Yes
Subularia aquatica	No ...	Yes ...	Yes
Sagina subulata	No ..	No ...	Yes
Cerastium Edmonstonii... ...	No ...	No ..	Yes
Arenaria rubella	No ...	No ...	Yes
Hypericum quadranulum ...	No ...	Yes ...	No
Geranium sylvaticum	Yes ...	Yes ...	No
Rosa mollis	Yes ...	Yes ...	No
Alchemilla filicaulus	Yes ...	No ...	Yes
Sibbaldia procumbens	No ...	No ...	Yes
Dryas octopetala	Yes ...	No ...	No
Saxifraga stellaris	Yes ...	Yes ...	No
Callitriche hamulata	Yes ...	Yes ...	No
Callitriche stagnalis	Yes ...	Yes ...	No
Epilobium alsinifolium	No ...	No ...	Yes
Cornus suecica	Yes ...	No ...	Yes
Matricaria phæocephala... ...	No ...	Yes ...	Yes
Taraxicum spectabale	No ...	No ...	Yes

Name of Plant.	Orkney.	Caithness.	Shetland.
Campanula rotundifolia ...	No ...	Yes ...	Yes
Lysimachia nemorum	Yes ...	Yes ...	No
Myosotis palustris	Yes ...	Yes ...	No
Rhinanthus grœnlandicus ...	No ...	No ...	Yes
Euphrasia borealis	No ...	Yes ...	Yes
Salix phylicifolia	Yes ...	Yes ...	No
Tofieldia palustris	No ...	Yes ...	No
Potamogeton alpinum	No ...	Yes ...	No
Saxifraga hypnoides	Yes ...	Yes ...	No
Potamogeton prælongus... ...	Yes ...	Yes ...	No
Juncus Balticus	No ...	Yes ...	No
Luzula spicata..	No ...	Yes ...	Yes
Carex salina	No ...	Yes ...	No
Agropyrum junceum	Yes ...	Yes ...	No
Polystichum lonchitis	Yes ...	Yes ...	No
Phegopterus Dryopteris ...	No ...	Yes ...	Yes
Lycopodium annotinum... ...	Yes ...	Yes ...	No
Isoetes echinosporum	No ...	No ...	Yes

The instructive lesson we hereby learn from the remarkable similitude of the floras accords with what geologists tell us, and with what botanists have said regarding similarly situated islands and continents. We know that if the land level were raised a few hundred feet, all the islands to the north and west of Scotland would form part of the mainland. We have positive proof that sea-beaches have been 50, 100, 150, and even 450 feet higher than at present, as seen on the west coast of Scotland. In Orkney, we have proof of earth movement in an opposite direction, and both prove the frequent fluctuations of land and sea-levels in past geological times. The remains of peat mosses of considerable extent have been found in several parishes as low as mean ebb tide. Investigations would no doubt show that it extends much farther. If the land were raised a few hundred feet we would have what would account for the unity of the flora in the north of Scotland. The flora of Caithness does not differ more from that of Orkney than it does from that of Sutherland. Mr Arthur Bennett, F.L.S., has taken great trouble to keep a reliable record of the floras of the different counties, and no doubt further investigation will bring the floras in still closer harmony.

SOME INTERESTING BOTANICAL FACTS.

The study of botany reveals some very interesting features of plant life, a few of which we may here specify. Some plants are glabrous, and this is more especially the case with aquatic plants, to which a covering of hairs would be a great encumbrance. Many land plants are covered with hairs. Some have the hairs adhering to the stem and leaves, whilst others do not. It is thought that hairs pointing downwards form a protection to the plant against injurious insects. These cannot climb the stem if thus protected, and hence the pollen and pistil are not interfered with—the reproductive parts of the plant. It is well known that leaves on land plants have many stomata on their underside. These mouths allow the carbon-laden air to pass in with its feeding properties, and the oxygen, of which the plant has a superabundance, to pass off. These are important functions, which, when interfered with, retard the growth of the plant. Now it is believed that in a climate such as ours, with a large number

of foggy days—cold, clammy fog—these stomata are
clogged and prevented from performing the process
of breathing. Nature comes, as she so often does,
to the rescue. A liberal coating of hairs tends to
prevent the clogging of the stomata, and hence
healthy plants are thus produced. One can observe
a tendency in native plants to have this growth increased. Mention may be made of a few. *Anthriscus
sylvestre* has a hairy stem in Orkney, and is glabrous,
as described in botanical books. *Jasione montana*
is hairier in Orkney. Then in Walls, Dr Fortescue
reports that *Calluna vulgaris* appears in some parts
as a hairy variety. Such are a few of the many
species that Nature seems to take under her pro-
tecting care. Some plants, as *silene inflata* and
Polygonum amphibium are glabrous in damp, and
hairy in dry situations. These hairs are also safe-
guards against too rapid evaporation.

All round our coasts there are succulent plants
—plants with thicker leaves. Succulent leaves are
said to retain their moisture longer, and are thus
suited to dryer areas. Some plants have their leaves
so much altered by the influence of the sea as to
form new varieties. *Euphrasia maritima* (Hook.)
and *Plantago maritima*, var. *linearis*, are cases in
point. Animals do not care for these leathery leaves,
and consequently there is a large survival of plants so
constituted. Anyone who has noticed a considerable
area of *Kakile maritima* will have noticed that these
tempting plants are seldom touched, unless provender
is short. Last summer the rabbits in this neighbourhood—and they were abundant—seldom touched the

plant till the grasses in the pastures were thoroughly eaten up. Then, but not till then, the *Kakile* was eaten to the ground.

There is no more interesting phase of botany than the sense-organs of plants. Plants feel, Linnæus said long ago. The movements of plants, especially the sleep of flowers and leaves, and the circumnutation of climbing plants are wonderful, for all such movements imply sensitiveness. The tentacles of our *Drosera* are marvels of sensitive organs. Place the tiniest bit of meat or midge on the centre of the leaf, and these finger-like processes will gradually curve round and locate the food accurately, and pour an acid on it which gradually dissolves the parts which are soluble. It is said that a bit so small as to be imperceptible when placed on our skin, is felt by the *Drosera*, and its digestive organs are set to work to feed on it.

Then Nature has made rare provision to prevent plants from interbreeding. Plants are stronger when they are crossed—when the pollen of one plant is used to fertilise the stigma of a plant of the same species on a different flower. Much of this is done by bees and moths, but provision to overcome this difficulty is otherwise made. Flowers have been classified as fertilised by insects—entomophilous—or by wind—anemophilous—and have wonderful adaptations to prevent the deteriorating effect of self-fertilisation. Everyone is acquainted with the disastrous results of in-breeding among animals. It is the same with plants. In this county we have three primroses. Two are yellow-flowered, and one pale lilac. All are dimorphous—that is to say if a number of specimens are examined, it will be found that about half have the stigma at the top of the tube and the stamens half-way down; whilst the other half have, on the contrary, the stamens at the top of the tube and the stigma half-way down. This has long been known and distinguished as "pin-eyed" and "thrum-eyed." Although this had been noticed for long, it was reserved for the genius and perseverance of Charles Darwin to explain the significance of this curious phenomenon, and its importance in the economy of flowers. Now after being pointed out, it is quite obvious. When an insect thrusts its proboscis down a primrose of the long-styled form, it cannot fail to deposit some of the pollen carried from other primroses on the stigma. Most flowers require crossing, and we find the machinery used of the most unexpected and complex description to prevent self-fertilisation and induce crossing. In proportion to the brilliance of the corolla or the sweetness of the perfume, is the need the greater for crossing. Inconspicuous flowers are either self-fertilised or only occasionally crossed.

THE GEOLOGY OF ORKNEY.

HE geology of Orkney in its main outlines is not of a very complex type. Practically the entire county is underlain by the Old Red Sandstone, and of this geological formation, two divisions are represented—the Middle (also known as the Orcadian) and the Upper Old Red Sandstone. Older rocks, principally granite and mica schist, form a small area near Stromness; and especially in Hoy and Deerness there are local outcrops of volcanic material. In these respects Orkney bears a close resemblance to Caithness, and in both counties flagstone is by far the most wide-spread rock. The flat contours and gentle slopes that characterise the landscapes are equally well marked in both counties. Shetland, on the other hand, is far more varied in its scenery and geological structure, though on both sides of Shetland the Old Red Sandstone spreads over considerable areas.

The Orcadian or Middle Old Red Sandstone, to which the flagstones belong, is known to be a fresh-water deposit laid down in extensive lakes which were inhabited by many species of fishes, though no marine animals peopled its waters. Its exact limits cannot be defined, but we can trace the old shore lines through a considerable distance in the west and south of Caithness. It is certain also that the lake extended south to Inverness, Cromarty, and Banff, and possibly to the town of Aberdeen, for the red sandstones on the south side of the Moray Firth contain the same species of fossil fishes as the grey and black flags of Stromness. The Old Red Sandstone of Shetland, however, apparently belongs to a distinct and later deposit.

Two features of the Orcadian Old Red are especially striking, firstly, the enormous thickness of the muddy sediments that gathered in the old lake, and, secondly, their great uniformity in character through what must have been a vast period of time. It was estimated by Sir Archibald Geikie, and recent surveys have confirmed his conclusions, that the pile of Old Red sediments ir Caithness is not less than 18,000 feet thick. At the bottom they rest on the crystalline and metamorphic rocks of the north-east Highlands, such as granite, gneiss, mica schist, and quartzite. The lowest beds are conglomerates and breccias, with red sandstones and mudstones, after which the flagstones were laid down which underlie the town of Wick and a considerable part of the south-east of Caithness. The latter are supposed to have no representatives in Orkney, but the superjacent beds that form the north and north-east of Caithness extend northwards across the Pentland Firth. It is true that in Orkney the granite floor rises through the flagstones at Stromness, and is covered by beds of conglomerate

which were originally the beach gravels that encircled
a granite islet, but these conglomerates are at a
high level in the sequence, and do not correspond in
position with those that occur in great thickness
around Berriedale and in Morven and Maiden Pap
in the south of Caithness.

The West Mainland of Orkney contains the oldest
rocks that occur within the boundaries of the county,
if we leave out of consideration the Stromness granite
and gneiss, which are of vastly greater antiquity than
any of the Old Red Sandstone deposits. The dark
grey flagstones of Stromness, Sandwick, and the west
of Birsay contain a group of fossil fishes which belong
to a lower horizon in the stratigraphical sequence than
those found in the rocks of the East Mainland and
the North Isles. The Stromness beds with the fishes
entombed in them correspond in age to the Achanarras
beds of Caithness, and to the sandstones of Cromarty,
Inverness, and Banffshire. The East Mainland and
North Isles are in part underlain by flagstones of
the same age and containing the same fishes as the
flagstones of Thurso. Still higher in the Orcadian
Old Red Sandstone are the yellow and red sandstones and the dark-red clays or marls that occur
near Roeberry, in South Ronaldshay; and in
Deerness, Shapinshay, and Eday. These are distinguished not only by their lithological characters,
but also by the occurrence in them of a distinct
assemblage of fossil fishes. The rocks of this group
were first proved to be fossiliferous by Charles Peach,
who investigated them at John O'Groat's, in Caithness, and since then have been known as the John

O'Groat's beds. In Orkney they contain flows of dark basaltic lava and beds of greenish volcanic ash.

The Middle or Orcadian Old Red Sandstone of Orkney, then, may be divided into the following members :—

3. JOHN O'GROAT'S BEDS.—Principally yellow and red sandstones with red marls and some dark flags. Near their base there is a volcanic zone.

2. THURSO BEDS.—Principally grey flagstones, with very occasionally thin beds of sandstone.

1. STROMNESS BEDS.—Grey flagstones, sometimes calcareous; thin impure limestones; sandstones and grits at their base, resting on conglomerate beds, which in turn rest on the ancient granite and gneiss.

The thickness of this pile of sediment is probably not less than 7000 feet, though it represents only the upper half of the formation, as the lower beds of Caithness apparently are not known in Orkney. They are of fresh-water origin throughout.

After these rocks had been deposited a great time elapsed, during which they formed dry land and were exposed to the eroding action of the atmosphere, rain, and streams. They were folded into broad arches and troughs, which were gradually planed across and reduced to a nearly level surface. Then, by degrees, another lake was formed and occupied a large part of Orkney and of Caithness; in it sand accumulated, which now forms the highest hills of the county. The yellow sandstones of the hills of Hoy belong to the Upper Old Red Sandstone, and are the deposits of this second lake. Similar rocks occur also at Dunnet Head on the south side of the Pentland Firth. Their beds are nearly horizontal, but below them the grey flagstones of the Stromness beds are seen dipping steeply to the west in Hoy Sound. The Upper Old Red Sandstone rests on the tilted edges of the Middle Old Red beds, which had been worn down to form a platform; the unconformability between the two series is consequently very marked.

From the point of view of the botanist, the geological structure of the Orkneys and the history of the rocks are of less importance than the nature of soils and subsoils and the configuration of the county. By far the commonest of the Orcadian rocks is flagstone, a type which is found in large development only in Orkney, in Caithness, and on the east side of Shetland. The Orcadian flagstones are fine grained dark grey rocks, which, though not hard, are often distinctly brittle. They contain a large percentage of clay and fine worn particles of white mica, but most of them have an admixture of sand, and they are nearly always somewhat calcareous. Their weathered surfaces are generally yellow or brown, and on decomposition they become covered with a layer of clay from which the lime has been removed, while the iron has become completely oxidised. The flagstones, however, are far from uniform in character. Many are quite arenaceous, and may be described as argillaceous sandstones. Occasionally we find beds of flagstones so calcareous that they have been burned for lime, but there are no pure limestones in the Old Red Sandstone of Orkney. Other flagstones consist so largely of clay that they might be described as dark shales, but they are not laminated. In the face of the cliffs the hard sandy beds weather out as prominent bands, while the soft shales or "calm-stones" are eaten back by the weather and form recesses. Beds which contain much carbonate of lime are comparatively rare.

SOIL FORMATION.

Where the flagstone beds weather they are readily broken up by the frost, because their bedding is exceedingly perfect, and they are also traversed by numerous joints. The subsoil in such a case is a rubble of loose rock fragments embedded in a fine brownish clay that represents the most weathered part of the subjacent rock. Although the soil is clayey it is well drained, and there is little tendency for water to be held up at the surface. The flagstones also are often sandy, and always somewhat calcareous ; they contain phosphates, both in mineralized state (as apatite), and as the teeth, scales and bones of fishes. Hence the soil is of mixed character, and may be described as a clayey loam, not devoid of lime, and fairly well provided with potash and phosphates. Although not a rich soil, it is by no means a sterile one. Soils of this kind are to be found over a large part of the county, especially at moderate elevations, where there is no great surface accumulation of boulder-clay or alluvium. At the highest elevations the flag-

f

stone soils are often modified by the presence of peat. The flagstone soils, however, are always thin, and the rocky subsoil is generally only a few inches below the surface. This ensures good drainage, but is in other respects a drawback, and neither for a cultivated nor for a natural flora do these soils prove very productive.

The next in importance to flagstone among the Orkney rocks is sandstone, which occurs mainly in Eday, Burray, South Ronaldshay, and Hoy. The John O'Groat's sandstones are always calcareous, and they are sometimes stained dark red with iron oxide. The soils derived from the weathering of these sandstones are naturally more porous than those formed on the flagstones, and they seem to be of inferior fertility, though they cover no great area except in Burray and Eday, where a large part of the sandstone districts is left uncultivated, and gives rise only to a rank growth of heather.

In Hoy also the Upper Old Red Sandstone seems to produce a barren soil, for over its whole extent there is very little cultivation. This may, however, be partly due to the elevation of the ground, as the Upper Old Red there forms a range of flat-backed hills, most of which is above the altitude to which cultivation is carried in Orkney. The same characteristics mark the area of these rocks that occurs at Dunnet Head, in Caithness.

The granite and gneiss of Stromness, and the volcanic rocks of Deerness and the North Isles, occupy so small a part of the surface of the county that it is hardly necessary to consider the peculiarities of the soils that arise from them.

BOULDER CLAY.

The "drifts" or loose deposits that overlie the rocks
are of the greatest importance as determining the
soils and agriculture of Orkney. Of these by far the
most wide-spread is the "boulder-clay," a glacial
deposit that covers most of the lower grounds. No
accurate maps have as yet been made to show the
distribution of the drifts, but it is probably a safe
estimate that boulder-clay occupies one-third of the
area of the islands. It varies in thickness from a foot
or less up to forty feet and more. Cliffs of boulder-
clay are to be seen at the east side of Kirkwall, the
north of Shapinshay, in Deerness, and in many other
places. Some of them are thirty feet high, but the
deposit may be much thicker than this, and, in default
of borings, it is impossible to estimate definitely what
may be its maximum thickness. In its distribution
there is one main characteristic, viz., it is confined to
the lower grounds and seldom occurs in continuous
expanses at elevations exceeding 250 feet. Consequently, on most of the hilly ground the soil is thin
and derived from the decomposition of the underlying
rock. Below that altitude, however, the reverse holds
good, and boulder-clay, usually only a few feet thick
is almost universal. Its presence may be observed in
the shore sections, on the banks of streams, and in
quarries and artificial openings of all sorts.

The boulder-clays of Orkney are seldom sandy or
loamy, and yield stiffish soils, which tend to be wet in
winter unless they are drained. On the other hand
they are generally calcareous, because they are

largely derived from the grinding up of flagstones in which carbonate of lime is present in considerable amount, and also because they contain shells and calcareous rocks that have been transported from sources outside the county. In this respect they resemble the shelly or calcareous boulder-clay of Caithness, with which they agree also in origin.

ICE AGE.

To understand the varieties of the Orkney boulderclays it will be necessary to give a brief account of the manner in which they are formed. It has been clearly proved that at the climax of the Ice Age the north of Scotland was covered by an ice sheet several thousand feet thick. The North Sea also was completely occupied by ice derived principally from the high land of Scandinavia. The Scotch ice was moving slowly down the eastern slopes of the Highlands into the North Sea, but there it was met by the Scandinavian ice, which, being in far greater volume, overmastered it, and forced it to turn backward over Orkney and the north-east of Caithness to escape finally into the Atlantic. Orkney was accordingly glaciated at this period by a thick sheet of ice that came originally from the basin of the Cromarty Firth, and after passing for a distance over the floor of the North Sea, was impelled north-westwards across the islands. In its progress it brought with it fragments of Highland rocks, of the Secondary strata around Brora, in the east of Sutherland, and many varieties of rocks and shells from the sea bottom to the southeast of Orkney. These all occur in considerable numbers in the boulder-clay ; the shells are usually striated and broken ; though sometimes single valves may be found whole.

By far the larger number of the rock fragments that occur in the boulder-clay, however, are of local derivation, and belong to varieties of rock that are common in the islands, such as flagstone and sandstone. They have all been transported from a greater or smaller distance, and consequently the boulder-clay is not strictly similar in composition to the rock on which it rests. In Westray, for example, there is often much sandstone, derived from Eday, in the boulder-clay ; and this is also the case near Kirkwall and in the East Mainland. The presence of shell fragments and of sand and silt from the sea-floor also makes the clay somewhat different from what it would be if it were entirely of local derivation. For these reasons it varies a good deal in different parts of the islands, but it is always a stiff, stony, unstratified clay, somewhat calcareous and of mixed origin, and the best soils on the islands are derived from this clay where it has been improved by artificial drainage and long cultivation.

The later phases of the Ice Age have left few traces in the Orkney Islands except that at the mouths of the higher valleys small conical or crescent-shaped moraines may often be seen, but there are no extensive sheets of fluvio-glacial sand and gravel such as cover enormous tracts in Sutherland, Ross, and Inverness. There are also none of the raised beaches which are so characteristic features of the shores of the Cromarty and Moray Firths. After the ice melted there were small lochans on the irregular surface of the boulder-clay, and most of these are now occupied by alluvial silt often overlying thin layers of fresh-water marl. The streams are of insignificant size, but along their courses there are many flat alluvial meadows usually drained and cultivated. The small peaty lakes in the moors afford a nidus for a swamp flora. The larger fresh-water lochs are often held up by dams of clay, but some of them seem to be rock basins, as they discharge over rock, and there are no signs of an old outlet filled up with boulder-clay. They are all quite shallow, and the water in them is distinctly calcareous.

The principal post-glacial changes in the surface configuration of Orkney are the silting up of many small lakes, the erosion of narrow gorges through rock by some of the streams, and the invasion of parts of the sea coast by blown sand. The sea cliffs also have receded before the attack of the waves, especially on the west coast, but few data are available to enable us to determine how far.

In Sanday, as the name implies, there is a very large area covered by blown sand, and all the features of sandy links are there developed in great perfection. In Westray, Deerness, Burray, and South Ronaldshay, there are also fairly large sea-side links.

PHYSICAL FEATURES OF ORKNEY.

We may now consider the physical development of the Orkney Islands and the origin of the more important surface features of the county. This can only be done in a very imperfect manner by means of the data afforded by the district itself, and what is known of the history of the adjacent parts of Scotland; the lapse of time since the deposition of the Old Red Sandstone is so enormous, and so little evidence is available regarding the Secondary and Tertiary rocks in north-eastern Scotland, that we are very much in the dark regarding many chapters in the history of the islands. We know, for example, that an extensive land surface existed in the region between the period at which the flagstones were laid down and that to which the Upper Old Red Sandstone of Hoy belongs. Even before this there was a land surface of which the only trace now left in our area is the unconformability exhibited at the base of the Stromness conglomerates. But these physical features are long anterior to the development of the existing fauna of the archipelago, and do not remotely concern us in this connexion.

The most obvious feature of Orcadian topography is the existence of groups of islands with intervening sounds and straits, and the highly irregular configuration of the coasts. The beds of sandstone and flagstone in the different islands must at one time have been continuous, and their separation has accordingly to be attributed to some agent of erosion, which, by removing great quantities of rock, has excavated the valleys, sounds, and bays. It is fairly obvious that this cannot have been done by the sea, as marine erosion is practically absent in the sheltered bays; and, in fact, deposition is going on there fairly rapidly in some places, as is known, for example, by the necessity of dredging some of the harbours in order to prevent the accumulation of silt. There can be no doubt that in places the sea is actually attacking the land, as, for example, on the exposed west coast, especially in the Mainland and in Hoy, but this action produces a simple type of coast line with few indentations, singularly unlike the complex and sinuous coast that prevails in the islands as a whole. We must also allow that in sounds where there are rapid tides a considerable amount of scour may be going on which not only prevents the accumulation of sediment, but may be deepening the channels even where these consist of solid rock. This tidal erosion, however, is confined to a very few localities, and has taken only a small part in the development of the present configuration of the islands.

If we compare Orkney with Caithness we can see that all the main features of the two counties are strikingly alike. The low, gently swelling hills, with broad, open valleys between, and great flat plains at their feet, that characterise the north-east of Caithness, have their exact counterparts in Orkney. In Caithness we have a great plain which has been carved out of the soft flagstone almost entirely by the action of the atmosphere, weathering, rain and streams, and there is no reason to believe that the sea has taken an important part in its formation. Similarly in Orkney the scenery is essentially that of a great plain, but all its lower parts have been flooded by the sea. The bays and sounds are drowned valleys, and in the gentle submarine slopes and the long stretches of shallow water that girdle the islands, we have the low, flat plain which in Caithness lies at the base of the hills and forms a large part of the land surface of that country.

It seems reasonable to believe that at one time Orkney was joined to Caithness and formed a northern extension of the Caithness plains. Dr Crampton [1] has pointed out that the topography of Caithness and of Orkney have many points in common. In Orkney the main ridges of high land lie on the west side, in Hoy, Orphir, Firth, and Harray, and this seems to be a continuation of the Dorrery Hills and the main watershed of Caithness that passes out to sea at Dunnet Head. In Orkney, as in the north-east of Scotland generally, the high ground lies to the west. The distance, for example, from the main watershed at Wideford Hill to the east side of Stronsay and Sanday is very great compared with that to Breckness and the western coast. At one time a great part of the North Sea must have been dry land, and the insignificant burns of the east of Orkney flowed out across a plain now submerged, uniting gradually to form more and more important rivers, and ultimately mingling their waters with larger streams that gathered the drainage of the Rhine, the Elbe, and other rivers of north-western Europe.

The land stood for a long time at this high level (probably several hundred feet higher than at present), and the water-courses were gradually deepened and widened till the main features of Orkney, as we see them now, were developed. There is a good deal of evidence to show that the

[1] The Geology of Caithness, *Mem. Geol. Survey*, 1914.

epoch of erosion belongs to a comparatively late period in the earth's history, probably to the Pliocene. At any rate it was complete before the climate began to change, and with increasing rainfall and greater cold the conditions supervened that inaugurated the Ice Age.

HILLS AND VALLEYS.

The valleys and the hills, however, were carved out of a great plain, of low relief, that belonged to a still earlier set of geographical conditions. Anyone who ascends Wideford Hill or one of the Hoy Hills on a fine day can see around him many eminences that rise to nearly the same level. This varies from 800 to 900 feet on the Mainland to 1400 or 1500 feet in Hoy, and these hill tops are the remains of a great plateau that extends southward into Caithness and Sutherland. In Harray and Birsay there are wide level summits to the principal hills, which are the remaining parts of this plateau; this is also true in Hoy, but at Wideford Hill and in some of the Firth Hills the ridges are narrower and the old plateau is less easily recognised. Geological evidence which is available in several parts of the West of Scotland goes to prove that this plateau out of which the scenery of Orkney has been carved (as the wood-carver cuts a pattern in a block of wood) belongs to the Miocene period, which preceded the Pliocene.

These changes carry us back a long distance, and concern the botanist and plant ecologist only indirectly, as determining the relief of the land surface.

The ice sheets which followed wiped out all the flora of the islands, and when they melted left a surface which at first must have been destitute of vegetation. The history of the present flora dates from that time. Not much is known about it as yet, but there is sufficient evidence to prove that there have been considerable changes of climate and geographical conditions, all of which must have directly affected the flora of the islands.

It is not altogether certain at what period the great submergence took place that drowned the valleys of the old land surface, and converted Orkney into an archipelago of which the individual islands represent the hill tops of the previous period. Before the oncoming of the Ice Age, the land stood three or four hundred feet higher than at present, and was of course very much more extensive. It is possible that a considerable subsidence took place immediately before the ice sheets over-rode the islands. After the ice melted, the land was probably very much at the same level as at present, or perhaps a few feet higher. Along the east coast of Scotland, all the way south of Helmsdale, there are numerous raised beaches, but these are either absent or very badly developed in Caithness and in Orkney. The most important of these beaches are the hundred-foot, fifty-foot, and twenty-five-foot beaches, so called because they stand approximately at these heights above present sea-level. The hundred-foot is the oldest of these, and next to it the fifty-foot beach. They show that there have been periods since the Ice Age when the land was sunken to the extent marked by each

beach, and that upheaval has taken place in successive stages. The absence of these beaches in Orkney
goes to prove that the islands have at no time since
the Ice Age been more deeply submerged than at
present, and that the extent of dry land now is as
small as it has ever been since the ice sheets melted
away. It is quite easy for any one familiar with the
islands to see that this must be the case. In many
places, as, for example, between Kirkwall and Scapa.
there are necks of low land that, if once covered by
the sea, would have been converted into sounds
through which powerful tidal currents would course.
These currents would have scoured out all sand, clay,
and mud, and left a bare floor strewn with large
rocks, and fringed with gravel beaches. But no such
valleys can be found in Orkney at present, and we
may be quite sure that the sea has never invaded
these grounds. There is indeed some evidence to
show that subsidence is still going on, but this is not
satisfactory; and if it is in progress it is certainly
very slow.

We cannot assume, however, that Orkney has
never been more extensive since the melting of the
ice sheets than it is now. As a matter of fact, there
are very strong reasons which would lead to the
opposite conclusion. The raised beaches merely prove
that the land was at one time submerged and has
risen in stages. At each halt in the process of
elevation a beach platform was formed. It is quite
conceivable, however, that the movement was oscil-
latory, and that, for example, after the hundred-foot
submergence the land rose considerably, and then

sank again to the fifty-foot level, where a pause ensued for a time; or that, after the epoch of the twenty-five-foot beach, the sea may have receded a long distance and subsequently returned to its present level, and many geologists believe that this was actually the case.

BURIED FORESTS.

The buried forests show that some such process has been going on. Beds of peat with stools of trees are known to occur at low-water mark and below it in several parts of the islands, *e.g.*, Westray, Skaill Bay, Deerness, and Sanday. Those who have made a study of these deposits are convinced that the trees and peat grew where they are now found, and this must have taken place on a land surface. Accordingly these buried forests establish that there was formerly a higher level of the land throughout the islands. It is impossible to make excavations in the sea-bottom except when the water is shallow, and consequently we have very little information as to the seaward limit of these forests. Where large docks have been excavated in some parts of England, it has been found that forest-beds occur 40 or 50 feet below low-water mark. We know also that trawlers dredge up peat and wood far out in the North Sea about the Dogger Bank. Facts like these lead us to suppose that at one time trees may have been growing far beyond the present boundaries of the land. At the same time we must not forget that this is only hypothesis, and is not yet, so far as Orkney is concerned, definitely proved. Mr Clement Reid supposes that the submergence of which the buried forests give evidence may amount to seventy feet or more. Dr Peach informs me that he was told by the late Mr Traill that great blocks of peat are torn up by tides and storms from the bottom of the North Ronaldshay Firth, and that in some of the Shetland voes the fishermen bring up peat on the flukes of their anchors where the water is by no means shallow.

If we look at the charts of the North Sea, we find that an elevation of about 200 feet would connect Caithness with Orkney and convert part of the Pentland Firth into dry land. No buried forests have been found at so great a depth in the North Sea. If Orkney has ever been joined to the mainland of Scotland during post-glacial times, an elevation of nearly this amount must have taken place. Of course it might be argued that the Pentland Firth has been deepened by the scour of the strong tides that rush through it, but this action, which has undoubtedly gone on, would be confined to the narrow part of the strait, and there might have been a heaping up of sandbanks where the current slackens. Accordingly, this estimate gives us a fairly exact idea of the amount of elevation that would be necessary to join Orkney to the mainland of Scotland.

There are certain strong reasons that would lead us to believe that the strait had been inter-rupted by a land connection at least once since the ice that deposited the boulder-clay melted off the face of the Orkneys. Many wild animals are to be found in the islands, principally rodents, such as hares, rabbits, mice, and voles. It is said that in the peat-bogs there are also remains of deer, and in all the islands toads are abundant. These animals are so generally distributed that it is difficult to believe that the islands have not at one time been connected together by dry land, and for the same reason we may infer that this fauna migrated into Orkney from Caithness at some period when a direct land connexion was in existence. The distribution of the animals over the archipelago can hardly be accounted for on the hypothesis that they were all accidentally introduced into their present habitats at different times by fortuitous circumstances. Many naturalists believe that a study of the flora and fauna of the Færoes and Iceland proves that these were joined to Europe in post-glacial times by a land bridge that has long since gone down beneath the sea. Similarly Shetland may have been connected with Orkney, or even with some part of Europe.

The evidence on which these hypotheses rest, however, is not geological, but depends on the nature and distribution of the living animals and plants. Some peculiarities of the fauna of Orkney deserve further consideration in this regard. One of these is the presence of a species of vole not known elsewhere. This would tend to prove that the islands have been distinct from the mainland of Scotland for a very long time, whether we are to regard this vole as having developed from other voles since the islands were cut off, or as the survivor of a species that once inhabited Scotland also, but has become extinct everywhere but in Orkney. Another remarkable fact is the absence of certain animals that are common in Sutherland and Caithness. Thus the frog and the adder do not occur in Orkney, though the toad is found there in great abundance. It is difficult to explain this except on the hypothesis that the land connexion did not last a very long time; at anyrate, this argument has been advanced to explain the absence of snakes from Ireland.

Perhaps the Pentland Firth did not exist in its present form at the time when the ice melted away. It may have been a narrow valley which had been cut by some pre-glacial stream. At first the North Sea was full of ice, and the water that arose from the melting of the snow found an easy escape through the Pentland Firth at a time when the North Isles were still covered by ice of considerable thickness, which blocked the outlet in that quarter. In this way the Pentland Firth would be soon widened and deepened so as to become a formidable barrier to the passage of land animals northward from Caithness. Hence the meagre fauna of Orkney may represent only the first animals that succeeded in crossing before the way was barred. It is supposed that the English Channel took its origin in a similar manner.

PEAT DEPOSITS.

The fullest record of the history of the Orkneys in post-glacial times is contained in the peat deposits that cover so large a part of the islands. Except where it has been cut for burning or removed by cultivation, peat extends over the most of the interior. It may be roughly classified into hill-peat and bog-peat, the former swathing the irregular surface of the hills often right to their tops, while the latter occurs in flattish depressions which were at one time swamps or lochans. Hill-peat varies in thickness up to about six feet, but the bog-peat may be thirty feet or more in depth. Apart altogether from artificial interference, such as drainage, cultivation, and digging for fuel, it is clear that in many places the peat is wasting away by natural processes. This is well seen on the hill-tops, such as Wideford Hill, where the peat is worn and channelled, and the stones are peeping out through a thin and broken covering. On the summit of the Ward Hill of Hoy the bare stones are everywhere visible, and there are only thin scraps of peat. Yet there can be little doubt that at one time these places were covered with several feet of peat deposit. On the Harray Hills the summit peat is rent and torn with great open "hags" or channels, and in dry weather the peat crumbles down and is blown away by the wind. Similarly, near exposed cliff faces, as in Westray and Sandwick, the peat is always removed for a considerable distance from the margin of the cliff. This is due to the action of wind and sea-spray. Clearly, then, the present geographical and climatic conditions are not the same as those under which the peat was formed.

REMAINS OF PLANTS FOUND IN PEAT STRATA.

No investigation of the geology and botany of the Orkney peat has yet been made, such as Dr Crampton[1]

[1] C. B. Crampton, "The Vegetation of Caithness," 1912.

and Dr Lewis[1] have accomplished for Caithness and
Shetland. By means, however, of the results of their
work in the adjacent counties, we can formulate a
few conclusions regarding the changes of flora, of
climate, and of geographical conditions which must
have taken place in the extreme north of Scotland
since the peat began to be formed. We can infer,
for example, with extreme probability that if the
vegetation of Caithness or of Shetland at a given
period was such as flourishes only under arctic or
sub-arctic conditions, the climate in Orkney also must
have been severe; and conversely, if trees flourished
in the north and west of Shetland, there must also
have been extensive forest growths in the Orkneys.

Now in Shetland Mr Lewis has found that at the
base of the peat and resting on the glacial drift
there is in many places a layer of arctic plants.
The characteristic members of this flora are *Salix
herbacea* and *Salix reticulata*. This peat sometimes
lies directly on the boulder-clay, but in other cases
a layer of aquatic plants occurs beneath it, and
fragments of *Potamogeton, Menyanthes, Ranunculus,*
and *Equisetum* underlie the lowest Arctic Bed.
Pollen grains of *Pinus sylvestris* have also been
found below the surface of the boulder-clay. The
Arctic Bed, however, is the first important and
widespread formation after the disappearance of the
glaciers that covered Shetland.

Above the Arctic Bed there is peat, and at a

---

[1] F. J. Lewis, "The Plant Remains in the Scottish Peat
Mosses," *Trans. Roy. Soc. Edin.*, vol. xli., p. 699; vol. xlv., p. 335;
vol. xlvi., p. 33 ; vol. xlvii., p. 793.

higher horizon the remains of trees, especially *Betula verrucosa*, Ehrh., and *Corylus avellana*, form usually a well-defined layer. This is the lower Forest Bed; temperate woodland marsh plants occur in this stratum. Mr Lewis gives a list of the plants identified by him in this deposit :—*Ranunculus hederaceus, R. Lingua, R. flammula, R. acris, R. repens, Viola hirta* (seeds), *Lychnis diurna* (?) (seeds plentiful), *Hypericum pulchrum* (seeds not abundant), *Montia fontana* (seeds very abundant), *Potentilla Fragariastrum* (a few achenes), *Pyrus Aucuparia* (wood and twigs), *Arctostaphylos Uva-Ursi* (one seed), *Calamintha officinalis* (nutlets), *Ajuga reptans* (nutlets), *Myrica Gale* (twigs), *Alnus glutinosa* (wood and catkins), *Betula verrucosa* (wood, seeds, and catkin scales), *Carex paniculata* (very abundant), *Carex sp., Osmunda regalis* (sporangia).

A consideration of this list shows that the climate must have been very much more favourable than when the Arctic willow overspread the low grounds of Shetland.

When we consider more carefully the distribution of the lower Forest Bed in Shetland, some remarkable facts come to light. The remains of well-developed trees are found even in the most exposed situations, where it is impossible to grow trees at the present day, even with careful artificial shelter. They occur near the summits of the hills in the centre of the Mainland, and even in the island of Foula. The trees do not represent copses growing in sheltered valleys away from the coast, but appear in every district hitherto visited, and are just as well developed in the most exposed situations as in the valleys. The plants are all such as might commonly occur in a swampy deciduous wood in any part of southern Great Britain at the present time.

The Forest Bed is sometimes two feet or more in thickness, and is overlain by a layer of peat containing *Eriophorum* and *Sphagnum*. This is followed in turn by a second Arctic Bed a few inches thick. It occurs in nearly all the localities where the peat of Shetland has been investigated. *Salix herbacea* and *Betula nana* are found in this layer, but *Betula verrucosa* has now completely disappeared. This flora indicates that the climate had certainly undergone a change for the worse. The entire absence of the temperate plants of the Forest Bed can hardly be otherwise explained.

Above the second Arctic Bed there is peat formed of *Scirpus*, *Eriophorum*, *Sphagnum*, and *Calluna*. It is not stratified as a rule, and may be many feet thick. Sometimes this layer rests directly on a weathered surface of boulder clay, and there seems reason to believe that in such cases the older peat deposits had been eroded away, or the conditions may have been unsuitable for the accumulation of plant remains, before the upper peat was deposited.

In Foula, in the upper peat, a layer was discovered very rich in fragments of *Juniperus communis*. Its exact significance is doubtful, but Mr Lewis points out that it corresponds in position with the Upper Forest Bed of the mainland of Scotland, of which the characteristic tree is *Pinus sylvestris*.

Dr Crampton, as the result of a wide survey of

the peat-bogs in Caithness, gives the following as the general succession of the deposits :—

5. Moorland peat.
4. Pine forest layers locally in the centre of the county, but not on the highest part of the plateau nor on the coastal region.
3. Moorland peat with *Sphagnum, Eriophorum,* &c.
2. Birch layers widely spread in the county.
1. A basal layer of *Salix arbuscula.*

The second Arctic Bed of Shetland, which should occur between the two forest layers (2 and 4 of the above succession), has apparently not yet been recognised in Caithness. In the south of Scotland, however, this bed is well developed, and contains *Salix reticulata, Salix herbacea, Loiseleuria procumbens, Arctostaphylos alpina,* and other plants.

CONCLUSIONS.

Professor James Geikie,[1] in his investigation into the history of the Glacial Period, has arrived at certain general conclusions that are strongly supported by Mr Lewis's researches into the Scottish peat-mosses. In fact, we may say that the significance of the Forest Beds was first of all recognised by Professor Geikie. Many years ago he pointed out that the Forest Beds indicated a climate much more genial than the present climate of Scotland, while the

[1] "The Glacial Succession in Europe," *Trans. Roy. Soc. Edin.,* vol. xxxvii., 1902, p. 127. "The Great Ice Age," 3rd Edition, 1894. "From the Ice Age to the Present," *Scot. Geog. Mag.,* vol. xxii., 1906, p. 397.

peat beds between them marked the occurrence of colder and wetter climates. Each Forest Bed is the evidence also of a time when Britain had a wider extent than it has now, and we need no further proof of this than the buried forests that now are covered by the sea. He also traced the relation between these beds and the raised beaches. There is good evidence to show that the hundred-foot beach belongs to an epoch of cold conditions, for the shells that occur in the clay deposits of this beach are of Arctic facies. The fifty-foot beach also marks a time when the climate was less genial than it is now, as in the west of Scotland there were glaciers descending through the mountain valleys to sea-level at the time when that beach was being formed. But the fifty-foot beach rests on a buried Forest Bed in some parts of the estuaries of the Tay and Forth. This is probably the lower of the two Forest Beds that occur in the peat-mosses. Similarly, there are traces of an upper Forest Bed below the deposits of the twenty-five-foot beach. During the Forestian epochs the sea must have retreated to a considerable distance from our shores, and Orkney may have been joined to the mainland of Scotland, while Britain may have been united to Ireland and to the continent of Europe. In the intervening cold epochs, when the peat flourished greatly and the forests died out or retreated to the south—the "Turbarian" periods— the land sank to 100 feet and to 50 feet below its present level, and the raised beaches were formed. Simultaneously there was an increasing accumulation of snow and ice in the higher grounds of Scotland,

and glaciers filled many of the larger valleys. The Lower Turbarian, or period of the hundred-foot beach, was on the whole colder than the Upper Turbarian period.

All these changes must have had a very marked influence on the distribution of the plants in Orkney and the north of Scotland generally, and a great part of the history of the flora of the county lies stored up in the peat beds and Forest Beds, and will some day be more completely known than at present. The study of the peat-mosses, in fact, should show us the stages by which our flora has reached its present condition, and enable us to decide which plants are natives and which have been introduced by commerce or otherwise in recent times. It may also be possible to establish that many southern plants once common in Orkney are now absent, or can maintain their hold only where specially protected and encouraged, while on our highest hill-tops still persist the remnants of a flora that once covered a great part of the low plains, where now a different type of vegetation prevails.

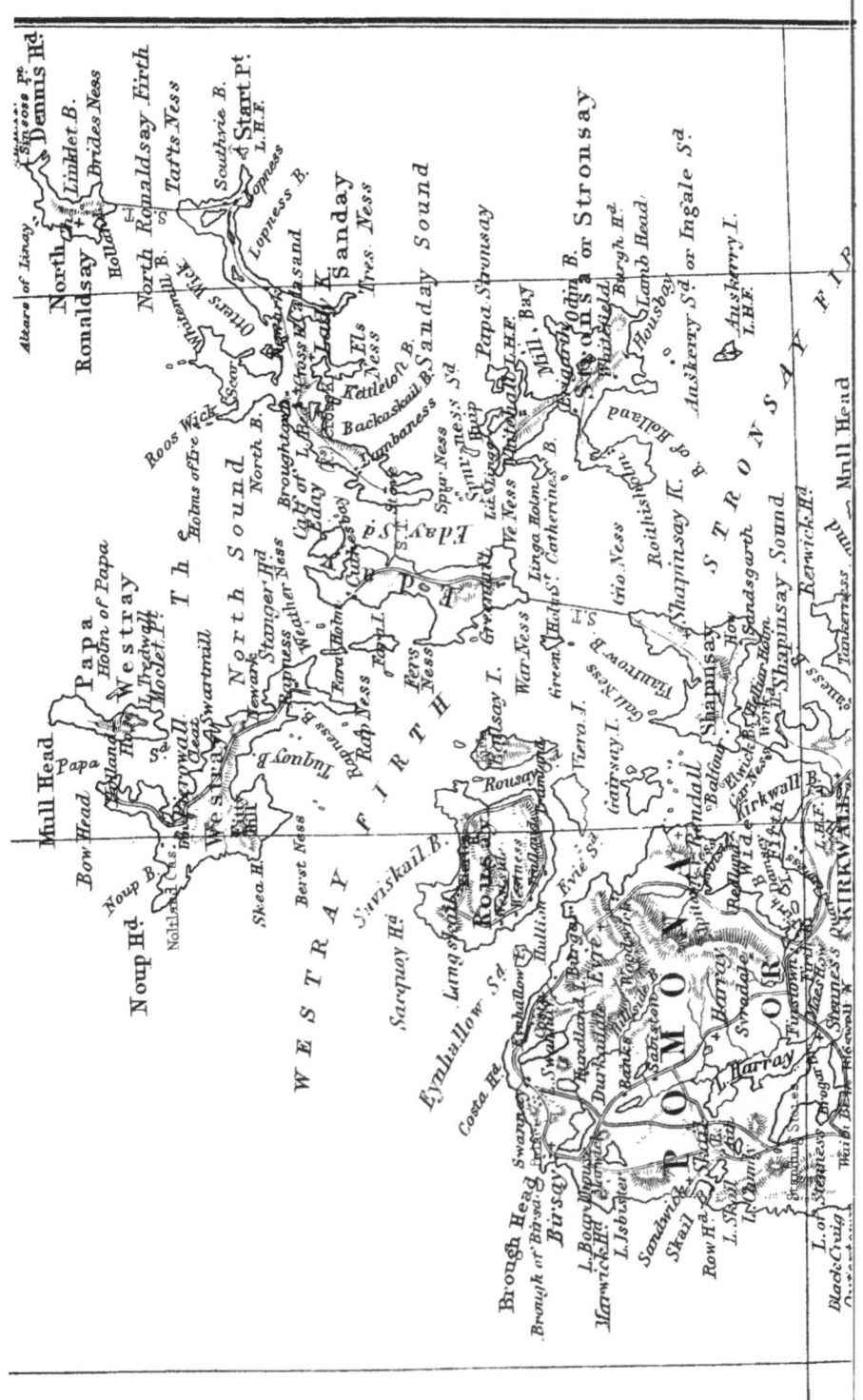

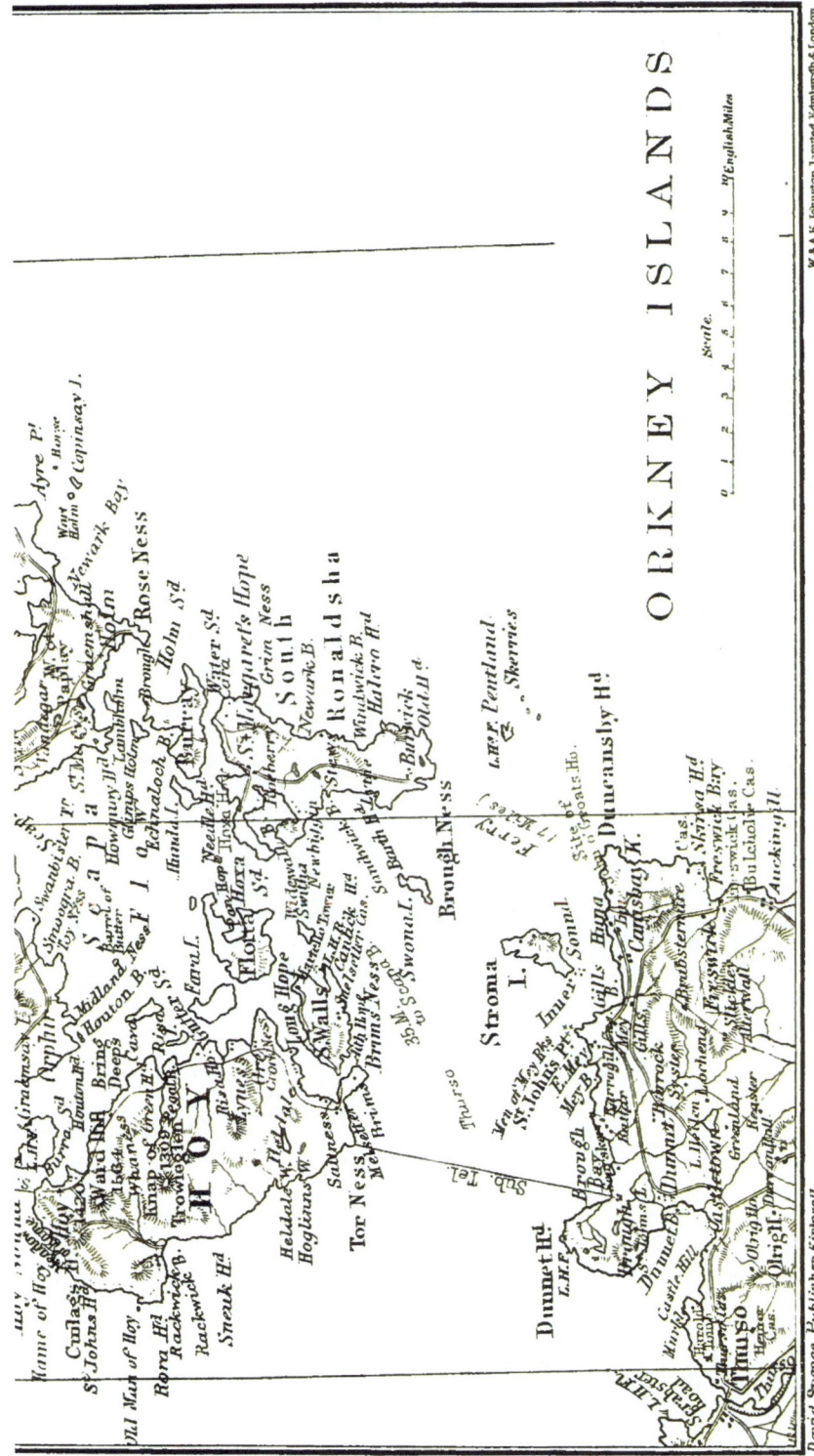

ORKNEY ISLANDS

Scale.

0 1 2 3 4 5 6 7 8 9 10 English Miles

W.&A.K. Johnston Limited Edinburgh & London.

David Spence, Publisher, Kirkwall.

FLORA ORCADENSIS.

CLASS I.—DICOTYLEDONES.

ORDER I.—RANUNCULACEÆ.

GENUS J.—THALICTRUM.

1. T. ALPINUM (Linn.), *Alpine Meadow Rue.*

This plant is local, but not uncommon, on several hills. It is found on the hills of Hoy, Orphir, Stenness, Evie, and Rousay. It is found occasionally at less than 100 feet above sea level.

2. T. DUNENSE (Dum.), *Lesser Meadow Rue.*

This is one of our rare plants. It is found on Links, Hoxa ; Links, Melsetter (Dr Boswell) ; at Dingeshowe (R. Heddle) ; Newark, Deerness (M. Spence) ; Links, Warsetter, Sanday (Messrs Scarth and Spence, 1909).

B

Genus II.—RANUNCULUS.

3. R. HETEROPHYLLUS. (Fries), *Water Buttercup.*

Quarry near Trumbland, Rousay (July 1907, M. Spence) ; Loch of Burness, Westray (July 1883, Col. H. H. Johnston, C.B.) No doubt in other localities.

4. R. BAUDOTII (Godr.), *Water Buttercup.*

Lochs of Brue, Lady, Sanday; and Burness, Westray (July 1883, Col. H. H. Johnston, C.B); Copinshay; Loch Bay and Millburn, Sanday ; bog, Mirkaday (Sept. 1909, M. Spence).

5. R. TRICHOPHYLLUS (Chaix), *Water Buttercup.*

R. Godronii (Gren.) is a variety with floating leaves. Quarry, Greentofts, Deerness ; Loch of Burness, Westray ; Lynnside, St. Ola (1874, Dr Fortescue). This plant is fairly common, and is to be found in several localities in addition to the above. (Seen by Mr Ar. Bennett.)

6. R. DROUETII (Schultz), *Water Buttercup.*

Dr J. T. Boswell, who says it is probably more common than the last, reports this plant from Swanbister. I have not a specimen, nor have I seen it growing. Loch of Aikerness (Dr Fortescue, 1882).

7. R. HEDERACEUS (Linn.), *Ivy-leaved Buttercup.* Rare.

Quendale, Rousay (R. Heddle) ; Papa Westray, in three localities (Messrs Scarth and Spence, Sept. 1909). The only locality where I met with this, in addition to above, was in Fair Isle, in July 1894.

8. R. Flammula (Linn.), *Lesser Spearwort.*
    Common.

f. pseudo reptans is a variety with arched internodes and rooting joints, which differs considerably
from sub-species *R. reptans*, which has not been
found in Orkney. This, I understand, is the designation given to this plant by Dr Boswell.

9. R. sceleratus (Linn.), *Celery-leaved Buttercup.*
    Very rare.

This rare plant was found by Dr Grant, Stromness, on the farm of Garson, near Stromness, in 1900;
he again visited the place on 31st August 1906, and
sent me a specimen. This is the only known locality.

10. R. acris (Linn.), *Upright Buttercup.* Common.
    (a) Steveni (Andrz.) Fairly common.
    (b) vulgatus (Jord.) Fairly common.

(a) Was reported by Prof. J. Trail in "An. of Scot.
Nat. Hist.," July 1908.

11. R. repens (Linn.), *Creeping Buttercup.*
    Common.

12. R. bulbosus (Linn.), *Bulbous Buttercup.* Not
    common.

Sandy links (Dr Duguid); Melsetter (R. Heddle);
sandy links, Deerness, St. Andrews, and Hoy (M.
Spence).

13. R. ficaria (Linn.), *Lesser Celandine.* Common.
Var. *divergens*. This variety is the more general

form in Deerness, but I am not sure whether this holds throughout Orkney or not.

Genus III.—CALTHA.

14. C. palustris (Linn.), *Marsh Marigold.* Common.

I have not found any of the varieties of this plant in Orkney.

Order II.—PAPAVERACEÆ.

Genus IV.—PAPAVER (Linn.)

15. P. dubium (Linn.), *Poppy.* Not common.

Evie (Dr Duguid), sandy cornfields, Kierfiold, Sandwick; and Deerness (M. Spence)— a very local weed of cultivation.

16. P. Rhœas (Linn.), *Poppy.*

This is given in R. Heddle's list as found at Westness, Rousay. Probably only where introduced. I have a poppy from a sandy field on the farm of Holland, North Ronaldshay, which resembles this. I have a specimen gathered by Dr Flett in Fife. The North Ronaldshay plant is nearer it than *dubium*, but agrees in details with neither.

Order III.—FUMARIACEÆ.

Genus V.—FUMARIA (Linn.), *Fumitory.*

17. F. capreolata (Linn.) Common.

18. F. purpurea (Pugsley), *Fumitory.*

This plant is reported by Prof. Trail in the July

No. of "Annals of Scot. Nat. Hist." for 1908, per Mr
Ar. Bennett.

19. F. BORÆI (Jord.), *Fumitory*. Common.

20. F. OFFICINALIS (Linn.), *Common Fumitory*.
Common.

ORDER IV.—CRUCIFERÆ.

GENUS VI.—NASTURTIUM.

21. N. OFFICINALE (Groves), *Water-Cress*. Several
places; local, but not rare.

22. N. PALUSTRE (Mœnch), *Water-Cress*.

This is a very rare plant, and has been found only
in Loch Ancum, North Ronaldshay. I gathered it in
Sept. 1908, when it was in fair abundance in west
end of the loch. It had not been found previously
farther north than Perth and Argyle. (See "Annals
of Scot. Nat. Hist.," No. 69, p. 53.)

GENUS VII.—SISYMBRIUM (Linn).

23. S. THALIANUM (Gay), *Hedge-Mustard*. Rare.

I found this on a wall top off King Street, Kirkwall, June 1895, and on the garden wall, Hoy Manse.

24. S. OFFICINALE (Scop.) Rare.

Church of Hoy (Dr Duguid and R. Heddle),
Swanbister; but probably introduced (Dr Boswell).

GENUS VIII.—CARDAMINE (Linn.)

25. C. PRATENSIS (Linn.), *Cuckoo-flower, Lady's-
smock*. Common.

26. C. HIRSUTA (Linn.), *Bitter Cress.* Local ; fairly common.

27. C. FLEXUOSA (With.), *Bitter Cress.*

Rarer than the last. Redland, Firth, 1901 ; no doubt in other places.

Genus IX.—CAKILE

28. C. MARITIMA (Scop.), *Sea-rocket.*

Fairly common in suitable localities on sandy shores. Shores —Evie, Deerness, Scapa, Hoy, &c.

Genus X.—RAPHANUS.

29. R. RAPHANISTRUM (Linn.), *Radish.* Common.

Genus XI.—BRASSICA.

30. B. ARVENSIS (Linn.), *Charlock.* Common.

This and the last are known in Orkney as " runshuk." The latter favours sandy soil, the former clayey.

31. B. RAPA (Linn.)

Var. *sylvestris* (Wats.) Little Sea, Lady, Sanday, naturalised (Col. H. H. Johnston, C.B.)

Genus XII.—BARBAREA.

32. B. VULGARIS (Br.), *Winter-cress.*

I found this behind Scapa Distillery in May 1898, and several on Quoybellock in 1899. Introduced with seeds no doubt.

Genus XIII.—DRABA.

33. D. VERNA (Linn.), *Whitlow-grass.* Fairly common.

34. D. INCANA (Linn.). *Twisted Whitlow-grass.* Rather rare.

Rousay hills; Syradale; Fitty Hill. The plant from Syradale I take to be the var. *contorta* (Ehrh.) Stems densely leafy, pouch glabrous.

Var. *minor* (Gray). This plant was sent me by Mr Ed. McKay, Westray, and gathered on Fitty Hill in 1910. It was examined by Mr Ar. Bennett, who named it as above.

GENUS XIV.—COCHLEARIA.

35. C. OFFICINALIS (Linn.), *Scurvy-grass.* Common.

36. C. ALPINA, *Alpine Scurvy-grass.*

This was found by Col. H. H. Johnston, C.B., on top of Knucker Hill, Westray, July 1883. It is also recorded in Dr Fortescue's list, on the authority of Dr Boswell. I found it on the Wart Hill, Rousay.

37. C. GRŒNLANDICA (Linn.), *Scurvy-grass.*

Black Craig and elsewhere along the coast. It grows on tufty headlands. Gathered by Rev. E. S. Marshall in July 1900; by me several times since.

GENUS XV.—CAPSELLA.

38. C. BURSA-PASTORIS (Medic.), *Shepherd's Purse.* Common.

GENUS XVI.—THLASPI.

39. T. ARVENSE (Linn.), *Penny-cress* Rare.

Rousay (Dr Duguid), Braebuster, Deerness, and Greenwall, Holm (M. Spence, 1896); it is fairly abundant on these farms. Field near Grainbank, Kirkwall (Dr Fortescue, 1911).

ORDER V.—VIOLACEÆ.

GENUS XVII.—VIOLA.

40. V. PALUSTRIS (Linn.), *Marsh-violet.* Fairly common.

41. V. RIVINIANA (Reich.), *Wood-violet.* Common.

42. V. TRICOLOR (Linn.), *Pansy.* Common.

43. V. ARVENSIS (Murr.), *Field-pansy.* Fairly common.

ORDER VI.—DROSERACEÆ.

GENUS XVIII.—DROSERA (Linn.), *Sundew.*

44. D. ROTUNDIFOLIA (Linn.) Fairly common on peaty heaths.

45. D. LONGIFOLIA (Linn.), *Long-leaved Sundew.* Very doubtful. Dr Gillies reported it about 1820, and Dr Clouston in 1831.

46. D. ANGLICA (Huds.), *Great English Sundew.* This is fairly common. It is found in the bogs, Hoy ; peat moss, Hillside, Birsay ; and very plentifully in White Moss, St. Andrews. *D. longifolia* is not found farther north than 62 degs. N. latitude, whilst *anglica* extends as far north as the White Sea. *Longifolia* is found in Caithness.

ORDER VII.—POLYGALACEÆ.

GENUS XIX.—POLYGALA.

47. P. VULGARIS (Linn.), *Milkwort.* Common.

48. P. OXYTERA (Reich.), *Milkwort.* Fairly Common.

I have specimens which I believe to be this. Mr Ar. Bennet informs me that he has a specimen of it from Orkney, gathered in Rousay by Miss Webb, July 1896.

49. P. DEPRESSA (Wend.), *Milkwort.*

This was a plant gathered in Deerness and Hoy, and sent to Mr Ar. Bennett, who so named it. This is given by Sir J. D. Hooker as a sub-species of *P. vulgaris ;* but as a separate species, *P. serpyllacea* (Weihe), by Prof. Babington.

ORDER VIII.—CAROPHYLLACEÆ.

GENUS XX.—SILENE (Linn.), *Sea-campion.*

50. S. MARITIMA (With.) Common on the seashore.

51. S. ACAULIS (Linn.), *Moss-campion.*

Considerable quantities are growing on the scree of the rocky ledges of Hoy Hills, and on Skea Hill, near Fitty Hill, Westray.

52. S. CUCUBALUS (Wibel), *Bladder-campion.*

Found on farm of Keigar, Deerness, in 1904 ; introduced with seeds.

Genus XXI.—LYCHNIS (Linn.)

53. L. ALBA (Mill.), *White Campion.*

This plant is reported in Dr Forescue's list as probably introduced; but in 1899 I found it on the cliffs near Mull Head, and the year previous on the cliffs below Cutpool, Deerness, where I had some difficulty in securing it. It is native in both places. It is also growing in a ditch below U.F. Manse, Evie, where it is probably an escape. I found it on Stove, Sanday, Sept. 1909; and on Bu, Burray, Aug. 1911.

54. L DIOICA (Linn.), *Red Campion.* Common.

This flower favours sandy links and sandstone cliffs.

55. L. FLOS-CUCULI (Linn.), *Ragged Robin.* Common.

56. L. GITHAGO (Scop.), *Corn-cockle.*

This is probably introduced. For two years it grew in great profusion among rye on Newark, Deerness, but disappeared when rye was no longer cultivated. Reported from South Ronaldshay, Sanday, &c.

Genus XXII.—CERASTIUM (Linn.)

57. C. TETRANDRUM (Curt.), *Mouse-ear Chickweed.* Common.

58. C. SEMIDECANDRUM (Linn.), *Little Mouse-ear Chickweed.* Rare.

Reported by Dr McNab, which Prof. Trail confirmed in 1888. Specimen sent me by Dr Grant from Cava, South Isles, in 1912.

59. C. VISCOSUM (Linn.), *Mouse-ear Chickweed.* Common.

60. C. TRIVIALE (Link), *Mouse-ear Chickweed.* Common.

I sent a rather peculiar *cerastium* to Mr Ar. Bennett, who said it had the habit of a *stellaria*, and was an abnormal form, and suggested it should be entered as *f.* of *triviale.*

GENUS XXIII.—STELLARIA.

61. S. MEDIA (Vill.), *Common Chickweed.* Common.

62. S. APETALA (Ucria), *Chickweed.*
Below Newhall, Deerness. This plant has three stamens.

63. S. UMBROSA (Opiz), *Chickweed.*
Fairly common in Deerness. This plant is known by its acutely tubercled seeds.

64. S. GRAMINEA (Linn.), *Lesser Stitchwort.* Rather scarce.

65. S. ULIGINOSA (Murr.), *Bog Stitchwort.* Common.

GENUS XXIV.—ARENARIA (Linn.)
66. A. SERPYLLIFOLIA (Linn.), *Thyme-leaved Sand-wort.* Common.

GENUS XXV.— HONKENEJA (Ehrh.)
67. H. PEPLOIDES (Ehrh.), *Sea-purslane.* Common.

Genus XXVI.—SAGINA (Linn.), *Pearlwort.*

68. S. MARITIMA (Don.), *Sea-pearlwort.*

Fairly common on seashore, Swanbister (Dr Fortescue); below E.C. Manse, Deerness; and elsewhere. There is a much larger variety growing in Papa Westray. Var. *debilis* (Jord.) was sent me from Stromness Harbour by Dr Grant.

69. S. PROCUMBENS (Linn.), *Creeping Pearlwort.* Common.

Var. *spinosa* (Gibs.) This interesting var. was found by Dr Grant near Stromness.

70. S. NODOSA (Fenzl.), *Knotted Pearlwort.* Local, not common.

Var. *S. glandulosa* (Bess) The variety is the more common form.

Genus XXVII.—SPERGULA.

71. S. ARVENSIS (Linn.), *Spurrey.* Not common.

72. S. SATIVA (Bœnn.), *Spurrey.*

This form is much more common than the last.

Genus XXVIII —SPERGULARIA (Presl.)

73. S. RUBRA (Pers.), *Seaside Spurrey.*

The Ayre, Kirkwall (Dr Duguid); Stromness (Dr Grant, in Oct. 1898); Sanday (Dr Fortescue).

74. S. SALINA (Presl.), *Seaside Spurrey.*

Var. *neglecta* (Syme). Fairly common on muddy, gravelly shores. The var. is the more common form.

Swanbister (Dr Boswell); Sandside, Eday, (Sept. 1908, M. Spence).

75. S. MARINA (Wahl.), *Sand Spurrey.* Not common.

Shore near Græmeshall, July 1910; Tankerness, Braebuster, Deerness; and elsewhere; Wauk Mill Bay and Hoy (Dr Boswell).

ORDER IX.—PORTULACEÆ.

GENUS XXIX.—CLAYTONIA.

76. C. PERFOLIATA (Donn.)

This is a naturalised plant from North America. Col. H. Johnston, C.B., reports it from garden of Hall of Tankerness, April 1884.

77. C. SIBIRICA (Linn.)

This is a naturalised exotic from North America; now found in plantation, Binscarth, and elsewhere.

GENUS XXX.—MONTIA (Linn.)

78. M. FONTANA (Linn.), *Water Chickweed.* Fairly common.

Var. *major* (All.) In edge of small loch to west of St. Mary's Village, Holm; Stronsay; Burn of Ore, Walls, Hoy (1884, Col. H. H. Johnston, C.B.)

ORDER X.—HYPERICACEÆ.

GENUS XXXI.—HYPERICUM (Linn.), *St. John's Wort.*

79. H. PULCHRUM (Linn.) Common.

80. H. ELODES (Linn.), *March St. John's Wort.*

This plant is given by Mr P. Neil, in his tour through the islands, as being found in the valley between the Dwarfie Stone and Rackwick, Hoy. No doubt this is a correct record. A gentleman who was secretary to the Natural History Society, Edinburgh, could hardly have mistaken the plant. Some one may yet find specimens.

ORDER XI.—LINACEÆ.

GENUS XXXII.—LINUM (Linn.)

81. L. CATHARTICUM (Linn.), *Purging Flax.* Fairly common.

Var. *condensatum* (Lange). I found this on links, Papa Westray, and sent specimen to Mr Ar. Bennett, who decided it was the above variety (Sept. 1909).

82. L. USITATISSIMUM (Linn.), *Common Flax.*

This plant is sometimes found growing on the roadside. It grows well and produces pretty blue flowers. The seeds probably fall from merchant vans.

GENUS XXXIII.—RADIOLA (Hill.), *Flax-seed.*

83. R. LINOIDES (Roth.)

Fairly common. Deerness, Westray, Hoy, &c.

ORDER XII.—GERANIACEÆ.

GENUS XXXIV.—GERANIUM (Linn.), *Crane's Bill.*

84. G. SYLVATICUM (Linn.)

Pastures about Kirkwall (Dr Duguid and Mr R. Heddle). I have never found it.

85. G. PUSILLUM (Linn.), *Small-flowered Crane's Bill*.

Roadside near Noltland Castle, Westray, Sept. 1909. There was a large bunch with seeds ripe and flowers of a beautiful pale pink (Messrs G. W. Scarth and M. Spence).

86. G. MOLLE (Linn.), *Dove's Foot Crane's Bill*.

This is a common plant on good dry soil. Dr Boswell suggests that it has been introduced; but it is surely too common and widespread for this.

87. G. PRATENSE (Linn.), *Blue Meadow Crane's Bill*.

My specimen was gathered in the yard surrounding the church, Egilshay, by Mrs N. Spence, Kirkwall. Curious how it got there.

88. G. DISSECTUM (Linn.), *Dove's Foot Crane's Bill*.

Not so common as 86, but I have frequently met with it on Crantit, in St. Ola; Deerness (in several places); Orphir, &c.

89. G. ROBERTIANUM (Linn.), *Herb Robert*. Rare.

Between Loch of Carness and the sea. In plantation of Binscarth. Native in former; probably introduced in latter.

GENUS XXXV.—ERODIUM.

90. E. CICUTARIUM (L'Herit.), *Stork's Bill*.

A specimen of this was brought to me from a field on the farm of Greentofts, Deerness—most probably introduced with seeds. It is also given in Low's list.

Genus XXXVI.—OXALIS (Linn.)

91. O. ACETOSELLA (Linn.), *Wood Sorrel.*

Low found this growing in considerable abundance on Calf of Flotta in 1774. It is also found on Ryssa Little. In 1906, Mr Omond, Kirbuster, gathered specimens on the Orphir shore and sent me some. I have specimens too from Dr J. S. Flett, gathered in April 1893.

Order XIII.—LEGUMINOSÆ.

Genus XXXVII.—LUPINUS (Linn.)

92. L. NOOTKATENSIS (Donn.), *Blue Lupins.*

This plant grows luxuriantly on several open, gravelly heaths, and is spreading slowly but surely. It has the power of extracting nitrogen from the atmosphere, which, becoming fixed in the soil, produces grass on barren soils. Hobbister, Stenness; Lyking, Voy, and Warth, Sandwick; hill ground to south of Barony, Birsay. It is not native—not even of Great Britain.

Genus XXXVIII.—ULEX (Linn.)

93. U. EUROPÆUS (Linn.), *Gorse.*

Introduced, local, and found in most parishes.

Genus XXXIX.—CYTISUS (Linn.)

94. C. SCOPARIUS (Link), *Broom.* Scarce.

Above U.F. Manse, Stenness; valley east of Stoney Hill, Harray; Smoogro, Orphir, and elsewhere—introduced.

Genus XL.—ANTHYLLIS (Linn.)

95. A. VULNERARIA (Linn.), *Kidney Vetch.* Common.

Var. *maritima* (Koch). Specimens of this were gathered in Deerness and Firth in 1911.

Genus XLI.—MEDICAGO (Linn.)

96. M. LUPULINA (Linn.), *Black Medick.*

Not infrequent (Dr Boswell).

Genus XLII.—TRIFOLIUM (Linn.)

97. T. PRATENSE (Linn.), *Purple Clover.* Common.

Var. *sylvestre.* Given in Dr Fortscue's list on authority of Dr T. Boswell.

98. T. MEDIUM (Linn.), *Meadow Clover.* Common.

99. T. ARVENSE (Linn.), *Hare's Foot Clover.*

Fairly common in artificial pastures.

100. T. REPENS (Linn.), *Dutch Clover.* Common.

101. T. PROCUMBENS (Linn.), *Hop Clover.*

Fairly common in artificial pastures.

102. T. DUBIUM (Sibth.), *Lesser Yellow Clover.*

Fairly common; probably introduced, but found on natural pasture.

Genus XLIII.—LOTUS (Linn.)

103. L. CORNICULATUS (Linn.), *Bird's Foot Trefoil.* Common.

    (a) The common form has long, scattered hairs.

    (b) In *f. glandulosus* from North Ronaldshay, many of the hairs are glandular.

C

Genus XLIV.—VICIA (Linn.)

104. V. Cracca (Linn.), *Tufted Vetch.* Common.

105. V. sepium (Linn.), *Bush Vetch.* Rather local.
Var. *montana.* This is said to be found in Lyra-
dale, Redland. I have not seen it, and do not know
on whose authority it is given.

106. V. sylvatica (Linn.), *Wood Vetch.*

During a school excursion in 1909, we gathered
several plants of this in a field of oats on Gritley,
Deerness—no doubt introduced. Later in the same
year, Mr James Omond, Orphir, sent me plants
gathered on roof of house in Greenigoe, St. Ola.

107. V. hirsuta (Gray), *Hairy Tare.*
Found in fields, probably introduced.

108. V. sativa (Linn.), *Common Vetch.*
Cultivated fields—introduced.

Genus XLV.—LATHYRUS (Linn.)

109. L. pratensis (Linn.), *Meadow Vetch.* Common.
Var. *ovata* (Bab.) is found.

110. L. maritimus (Big.)
This plant is given in "Flora Scotica" and in
Hooker, 3rd Edit., as growing in Orkney. Var.
acutifolia is given for the Shetlands and Orkney.
Have never seen it.

111. L. montanus (Bernh.), *Earth-nut Pea.* Rare.
Found in the Burn of Ore, Walls (Dr Boswell and

R. Heddle). The above plant is better known as *orobus tuberosus.*

GENUS XLVI.—MELILOTUS (Hill).

112. M. OFFICINALIS (Lam.), *Melilot.*

This was found in field of Quoybelloch, Deerness; and old quarry, St. Ola, near Greenigoe; introduced in both cases. I find that Dr Flett reported it in 1890.

ORDER XIV.—ROSACEÆ.

GENUS XLVII.—SPIRÆA (Linn.)

113. S. ULMARIA (Linn.), *Meadow Sweet.*

Common in Orkney, and known as *Yule-girse.*

GENUS XLVIII.—ALCHEMILLA (Linn.)

114. A. ARVENSIS (Scop.), *Field Lady's Mantle.*

Fairly common in cultivated fields.

115. A. VULGARIS (Linn.), *Lady's Mantle.* Rather scarce.

Var. *montana* (Willd.) This is a dwarf form with silky leaves and petioles. I found this in July 1907 on Rousay Hill, above Trumbland. Col. H. Johnston reported it in 1876-77 on Midland Hill, Orphir.

Var. *filicaulis* (Buser). Same as above. This is reported in "Journal of Botany" and "Ann. Scot. Nat. Hist.," 1906.

Var. *pratensis* (Schmidt). "Journal of Botany, p. 111 in 1895; also "Ann. Scot. Hist.," July 1908.

A. vulgaris (Linn.) Some difference of opinion exists in regard to the varieties of this plant.

Rev. E. F. Linton, in a paper on the segregates of *A. vulgaris*, states that *A. montana*, (Willd.) is not British. In that case the variety in Orkney will be *A. filicaulis*. E. F. Linton, in "Ann. Scot. Nat. Hist.," p. 122, 1906, gives *A. filicaulis* (Buser) as found in Orkney, and it is one of the plants in *herbarium* of Dr Boswell.

Genus XLIX. –POTENTILLA (Linn.)

116. P. SILVESTRIS (Neck.), *Bark.* Common.

It is used in Orkney for dyeing nets, and medicinally as an astringent. Mr Ar. Bennett said that a variety sent him should be entered as the form known as *f. incisa* (M. Spence, July 1908).

117. P. ANSERINA (Linn.), *Silver Weed.* Common.

Genus L.—COMARIUM (Linn.)

118. C. PALUSTRE (Linn.), *Marsh Cinque-foil.* Common.

Genus LI.—POTERIUM (Linn.), *Burnet.*

119. P. SANGUISORBA.

Several of these were found in rye-grass of Quoy-bellock, 1904. No doubt sown with clover.

Genus LII.—FRAGARIA (Linn.)

120. F. VESCA (Linn.), *Wood Strawberry.* Rare.

Trumbland, loch behind Westness, and rocks, Rousay (Dr Duguid, Robert Heddle, and Patrick Neil). I have often looked for this plant but never found it.

Genus LIII.—RUBUS (Linn.)

121. R. FISSUS (Lindl.), *Bramble.* Very rare.

This is confined to one small spot at the South Burn of Quoys, Hoy. I gathered it in July 1902.

122. R. SAXATILIS (Linn.), *Stone Raspberry.*

Fairly common on rocky banks of streams and lochs.

Genus LIV.—GEUM (Linn.)

123. G. RIVALE (Linn.), *Water-avens.* Local and rather scarce.

124. G. URBANUM (Linn.), *Wood-avens.*

This grows in the plantation, Binscarth—introduced. Have not seen it anywhere else.

Genus LV.—DRYAS (Linn.)

125. D. OCTOPETALA (Linn.), *Mountain-avens.* Very rare.

North-west side of Hoy Hill (Dr Duguid and R. Heddle). My specimen was sent me by Dr Grant from Kame, Hoy.

Genus LVI.—ROSA (Linn.)

126. R. MOLLIS (Sm.)

Wauk Mill Bay (Dr Boswell).

Var. *cœrulea.* South Burn of Quoys, Hoy (Dr Boswell).

127. R. TOMENTOSA (Sm.)

Not common. My specimen was gathered in valley at foot of Syradale Burn.

Var. *subglobosa*. Redland Burn, Firth (1905, M. Spence).

128. R. CANINA (Linn.)

Var. *dumalis* (Bechst.) Burn of Quoys, Hoy, and Wideford Burn in 1902 (M. Spence) ; Searquoy Burn, Orphir (Dr Boswell).

Var. *Reuteri*. Oyce, Firth (Dr Boswell); Hoy (1875, Col. H. H. Johnston, C.B.)

Var. *subcristata*. Oyce, Firth (1880, Col. H. H. Johnston, C.B.)

Var. *lutetiana* (Leman). Crags at burn side, Ward Hill, Hoy (1883, Col. H. H. Johnston, C.B.)

GENUS LVII.—PYRUS (Linn.)

129. P. AUCUPARIA (Ehrh.), *Rowan Tree*.

This is confined to a few of the South Isles. It is often met with in the valleys of Hoy and Walls. A bush or two in Calf of Flotta.

ORDER XV.—LYTHRACEÆ.

GENUS LVIII.—PEPLIS (Linn)

130. P. PORTULA (Linn.), *Water Purslane*.

Local, but met with in several places—above Langskail, St. Andrews; U.F. Church, Orphir; School-house, Evie; bog, Mirkaday, Deerness.

ORDER XVI.—ONAGRACEÆ.

GENUS. LIX.—EPILOBIUM (Linn.)

131. E. ANGUSTIFOLIUM (Linn.), *French Willow*. Rare.

Rysadale, Stenness ; Trumland ; Dwarfie Stone ; Head of Holland.

132. E. PARVIFLORUM (Schreb.), *Small-flowered Willow-herb.* Scarce.

It grows below Upper Braebuster, Deerness, and near Hall of Tankerness (1899). Dr Grant found it same summer near Stromness; Myre, Sanday.

133. E. MONTANUM (Linn.), *Willow-herb.* Common.

134. E. TETRAGONUM (Curt.), *Square-stalked Willow-herb.*

Some doubt has been expressed as to whether this plant grows in Orkney ; but I believe it is to be found in several places in St. Andrews. The leaves differ much from *obscurum.* Mr Patrick Neil reports it from the Gills of Scapa.

135. E. OBSCURUM (Schreb.), *Willow-herb.* Fairly common.

Ward Hill, Orphir; St. Andrews—several places.

136. E. PALUSTRE (Linn.), *Narrow-headed Willow-herb.* Not uncommon.

Bog, Mirkaday, Deerness; Orphir, &c.

Var. *lineare* (Krause). This is a variety sent to Mr Ar. Bennett and named by him. Several crosses have been found among the *epilobiums.* I got one in peat banks to south of junction of Tankerness and Deerness roads—*Palustre* × *obscurum.*

Genus LX.—CIRCÆA (Linn.)

137. C. ALPINA (Linn.), *Enchanter's Nightshade.* Rare.

Hoy, Evie, Naversdale. I got fine specimens in Burn of Redland, Firth, in 1905; accidentally introduced at Swanbister.

Order XVII.—HALORAGACEÆ.

Genus LXI.—HIPPURIS (Linn.)

138. H. VULGARIS (Linn.), *Mare's Tail.*

In several streams—St. Andrews, Evie, Harray, &c.

Genus LXII. MYRIOPHYLLUM (Linn.)

139. M. ALTERNIFLORUM (DC.), *Water-milfoil.* Common.

140. M. SPICATUM (Linn.), *Spiked Water-milfoil.* Scarce.

In several parts of Loch Stenness, and in Loch Bea, Sanday; bog, Mirkaday, Deerness; specimens gathered in July 1898.

Genus LXIII.—CALLITRICHE (Linn.)

141. C. VERNALIS (Koch), *Water-starwort.*

Specimens were seen by Mr Bennet, and so named.

142. C. STAGNALIS (Scop.), *Water-starwort.* Common. Above School, St. Andrews, &c.

143. C. POLYMORPHA (Lönnr.), *Water-starwort.* Bog, Stove, Deerness.

144. C. INTERMEDIA (Hoffm.)

Bog, Stove ; Fidge, Swanbister (Dr Boswell).

145. C. AUTUMNALIS (Linn.), *Autumn Water-starwort.*

Loch Skail, small loch in Papa Westray, and St. Mary's Loch, Holm ; Wasbister, Rousay (G. W. Scarth).

ORDER XVIII.—CRASSULACEÆ.

GENUS LXIV.—SEDUM (Linn.)

146. S. ROSEUM (Scop.), *Stonecrop.*

Common on cliffs— Hoy Hill and Rousay.

147. S. ACRE (Linn.), *Biting Stonecrop.* Rare.

This plant is found only on the links, Hoxa, where it is scarce.

ORDER XIX.—SAXIFRAGACEÆ.

GENUS LXV.—SAXIFRAGA (Linn.)

148. S. OPPOSITIFOLIA (Linn.), *Mountain Saxifrage.* Rare.

Hoy Hills. I found one plant on the north-west side of Ward Hill. Crags on Ward Hill, Hoy (Aug. 1881, Col. H. H. Johnston, C B.)

149. S. STELLARIS (Linn.), *Starry Saxifrage.* Rare.

On rocks near Rackwick, Hoy (Dr Duguid). My specimens were gathered by Mr G. W. Scarth in gullies near Meadow of Kame in Aug. 1908.

150. S. HYPNOIDES (Linn).

This is given in Dr Clouston's list in Anderson's
" Guide to Islands of Scotland," as growing on Ward
Hill, Hoy.   Mr Ar. Bennett gives it as occurring in
Orkney and Shetland, in "Ann. Scot. Nat. Hist.,"
Jan. 1909.   Mr Pat. Neil says:—"As *S. hypnoides* is
entirely omitted from Mr Low's list, though pretty
common, I am inclined to think that this has been
mistaken for *S. cæspitosa*, which I did not observe in
Orkney."

151. S. AIZOIDES (Linn.), *Yellow Mountain Saxifrage.*

Fairly common on hills and in valleys, Hoy.   Mr
Ar. Bennett, in "Scottish Botanical Review" for
October 1912, says :—"Among plants from Orkney
sent me by Mr M. Spence are two specimens of
S. aizoides, and answering to the description of *f.
aurantia* of Hartmann, ('Vet. Ak. Handl,' 1818).
The leaves are orange, shading to yellow at the apex.
The lower stem leaves are suffused with red, and the
fruit is orange-red (half ripe).   The leaves are quite
entire, very thick, with here and there a long patent
hair.   This form occurs in Norway, with ordinary
form in Sweden."

GENUS LXVI.—CHRYSOSPLENIUM (Linn.)

152. C. OPPOSITIFOLIUM (Linn.), *Golden Saxifrage.*
Rocky banks of streams; local, but not rare.

GENUS LXVII.—PARNASSIA (Linn.)

153. P. PALUSTRIS (Linn.), *Grass of Parnassus.*
Common.

ORDER XX.—UMBELLIFERÆ.

GENUS LXVIII.—HYDROCOTYLE (Linn.)

154. H. VULGARIS (Linn.), *White-rot.* Common.

GENUS LXIX.—APIUM (Linn.), *Marsh-wort.*

155. A. INUNDATUM (Reichb.) Fairly common.

Ness, Campston, St. Andrews ; bog, Mirkaday, Deerness, &c.

GENUS LXX.—ÆGOPODIUM (Linn.)

156. A. PODAGRARIA (Linn.), *Gout-weed.*

Fortunately very local ; no doubt introduced. Hillside, Birsay ; Stromness, Kirkwall, Stenness, Deerness, &c.

GENUS LXXI.—CARUM (Linn.)

157. C. CARVI (Linn.), *Caraway.*

Local ; burn near Hestakelda, Holm ; meadows below Cletts, South Ronaldshay ; Westray (1905); naturalised in these places.

GENUS LXXII.—SISON (Linn.), *Stone Parsley.*

158. S. AMOMUM (Linn.)

This plant was found by Dr Grant at the roadside. I think it was in Stenness. It was a curious place in which to find such a plant, and raises the interesting question as to how it got there.

GENUS LXXIII.—BUNIUM (Linn.)

159. B. FLEXUOSUM (Fr.), *Pig-nut.*

This plant was very numerous in a grass park to the east of Warrenfield in June 1911, where I gathered several with unusually large tubers. The park had not been pastured on before June, and the field was almost white with the flowers of this. The tubers were more like potatoes than those in my herbarium gathered near Edinburgh by Dr Flett. Mr Ar. Bennett says of it, " I have never seen such a tuber. I can only think it is a very old tuber."

Genus LXXIV.—PIMPINELLA (Linn.)

160. P. Saxifraga (Linn.), *Burnet Saxifrage.* Rare.

Picaquoy (1899, M. Spence), Burn of Hatston (Dr Flett, 1890), Caldale, St. Ola (1912, M. Spence).

Genus LXXV.—SIUM (Linn.)

161. S. erectum (Huds.), *Water-parsnip.* Rare.

Burn running into Loch Ayre, Holm. I gathered specimens here in 1894. Mr Scarth brought plants of this from a small stream near Newark, Sanday, in Sept. 1909.

Genus LXXVI.—ÆTHUSA (Linn.)

162. Æ. Cynapium (Linn.), *Fool's Parsley.*

Fields, Rousay ; gardens, Kirkwall. I have never met with it.

Genus LXXVII.—LIGUSTICUM (Linn.)

163. L. scoticum (Linn.), *Scottish Lovage.* Fairly common.

Frequent along seashore of Mainland and several islands ; Gloup, Deerness ; Shapinsay ; Rousay, &c.

Genus LXXVIII.—ANGELICA, *Angelica.*

164. A. sylvestris (Linn.), *Wild Angelica.*
Common by sides of streams.

Genus LXXIX.—ARCHANGELICA (Hoffm.)

165. A. officinalis (Hoffm.)

This plant is found at roadside, village of Piero-wall, and Dr Grant found it in Stromness. It is probable that it has been brought to both places by Færoe smacks when landing fish. It is an abundant plant in the Færoes. It grows well in Westray. (See "Ann. Scot. Nat. Hist.," July 1908.) "In the Færoes this species is not only found in the cultivated parts, but in large masses, and very fine in the talus of the bird-cliffs, and also in small yards near the houses. It occurs in Iceland, too, 'here and there,' where it is also cultivated. It is said to be abundant in the northern parts of that island."—Mr Ar. Bennett.

Genus LXXX.—HERACLEUM (Linn.)

166. H. Sphondylium (Linn.), *Hogweed.*   Common.

Genus LXXXI.—DAUCUS (Linn.)

167. D. Carota (Linn.), *Wild Carrot.*

This plant is found pretty frequently in rye-grass fields—probably introduced.

Genus LXXXII.—CHÆROPHYLLUM (Linn.)

168. C. temulum (Linn.), *Chervil.*

Waysides, not common (R. Heddle). I have not met with it. It grows in Caithness.

GENUS LXXXIII.—ANTHRISCUS (Bernh.)

169. A. VULGARIS (Bernh.), *Beaked Parsley.*

Reported by Dr Duguid and R. Heddle.

170. A. SYLVESTRIS (Hoffm.), *Wild Beaked Parsley.*

Swanbister, not uncommon. It grows pretty frequently in the neighbourhood of farm steadings and at road sides in rich soil. Also recorded by Neil. Mr Bennett got specimens which he said were of this plant, but differed slightly. Mr Bennett—" It is a form that is not familiar to me at first sight. Opiz has a variety, *alpestre*, but gives no description."

GENUS LXXXIV.—FŒNICULUM (Hill).

171. F. VULGARE (Mill.), *Fennel.*

Grassy banks, seashore, Carrick, Eday (July 1883, Col. H. H. Johnston, C.B.) I failed to find this in 1908 ; probably extinct.

GENUS LXXXV.—SCANDIX (Linn.)

172. S. PECTEN-VENERIS (Linn.), *Shepherd's Needle.*

In cornfields ; rather scarce. Deerness, Firth, South Ronaldshay, Stromness, &c.

GENUS LXXXVI.—CONIUM (Linn.)

173. C. MACULATUM (Linn.), *Hemlock.* Scarce.

Mirkaday, Lingro, Berstane, Crantit, &c. Dr Fortescue writes, " I noticed last August (1911) that the *conium* had died out at the spot where I first observed it about 1880, and was now growing eighty yards farther west on side of public road, Lingro."

Order XXI.—ARALIACEÆ.

Genus LXXXVII.—HEDERA (Linn.)

174. H. Helix (Linn.), *Common Ivy.* Rare.

Recorded from Berridale, Hoy (Dr Boswell), and Rousay (Dr Duguid and R. Heddle). Dr Fortescue says, "I have since seen it on the cliffs at Berstane."

Order XXII.—CAPRIFOLIACEÆ.

Genus LXXXVIII.—SAMBUCUS (Linn.)

175. S. nigra (Linn.), *Elder.*

Kirkburn, Hoy—introduced.

176. S. Ebulus (Linn.), *Dwarf Elder.*

Wideford Burn—introduced.

Genus LXXXIX —LONICERA (Linn.)

177. L. Periclymenum (Linn.), *Honeysuckle.*

Rocks in Orphir, Walls, Hoy, and Rysa Little; Rousay (R. Heddle). Rev. G. Low says:—"This plant not only adorns the landscape in Hoy by its tufts of fine flowers, but scents it with its agreeable smell."

Order XXIII.—CORNACEÆ.

Genus XC.—CORNUS (Linn.)

178. C. suecica (Linn.), *Dogwood.* Very rare.

Dr Grant forwarded specimens to me which I understood were obtained at the foot of cliffs bounding the Meadow of Kame. Mr Bennett wrote that Mr Beeby found this in Shetland, but it has not been found in Caithness.

ORDER XXIV.—RUBIACEÆ.

GENUS XCI.—GALIUM (Linn.)

179. G. VERUM (Linn.), *Lady's Bedstraw.* Common.

Var. *maritimum* (DC.)   On dry links, Dingies-
howe and Newark, Deerness ; and no doubt elsewhere.
Specimens were sent to Mr Ar. Bennett in 1907.

180. G.   SAXATILE   (Linn.),   *Heath   Bedstraw.*
Common.

181. G. MOLLUGO (Linn.), *Hedge Bedstraw.*

Var. *Bakeri* (Syme).   Very rare.   I found one
patch about two feet square on the farm of Quoybelloch, Deerness, about 1895.   When the surrounding heath was cultivated, this, at my request, was
left, and is so at present.   When in Westray in
1905, I came across one or two patches above the
village of Pierowall.   (Examination confirmed by Mr
Ar. Bennett).

182. G. ASPERUM (Schreb), *Mountain   Bedstraw.*
Scarce.

Hoy Hill and Houton Head (Dr Boswell); Burn of
Sale, Hoy (R. Heddle); Holm Hill ; above school, St.
Andrews (M. Spence).   It is also given in " Journal of
Botany" in list called " Florula Orcadensis," on the
authority of Syme.

183. G. ULIGINOSUM (Linn.), *Rough Water Bedstraw.*

Reported by Low, but requires confirmation.   It
is found in Caithness, Hebrides, &c.

184. G. PALUSTRE (Linn.), *White Water Bedstraw.* Common.

Var. *Witheringii* (Sm.) Fairly common. In bog, Mirkaday, Deerness; Scapa (Col. H. H. Johnston, C.B., 1876).

185. G. APARINE (Linn.), *Cleavers.* Not uncommon on gravelly seashores.

GENUS XCII.—SHERARDIA (Linn.)

186. S. ARVENSIS (Linn.), *Field Madder.* Fairly common.

Fairly abundant in East Mainland. Some botanists say it has been introduced; but it it surely too abundant for this, in Deerness at least.

ORDER XXV.—VALERIANACEÆ.

GENUS XCIII.—VALERIANA (Linn.)

187. V. OFFICINALIS (Linn.), *Valerian.*

Not uncommon by sides of streams; (Dr Fortescue).

188. V. SAMBUCIFOLIA (Mikan). Fairly common.

Hoy, Ireland, and elsewhere. This is the more common species; the last is rare.

189. V. PYRENAICA (Linn.)

This grows in plantation, Binscarth; no doubt introduced.

GENUS XCIV.—VALERIANELLA (Mill.)

190. V. OLITORIA (Poll.), *Corn Salad.*

Fields (Dr Duguid). Evidently very rare. A

D

specimen was found in a herbarium purchased by H. C. Watson, Esq., which at one time was the property of Dr Gillies and collected in Orkney by himself and Dr Duguid.

ORDER XXVI.—DIPSACEÆ.

GENUS XCV.—SCABIOSA (Linn.), *Scabious.*

191. S. SUCCISA (Linn.), *Devil's Bit.*   Common.

192. S. ARVENSIS (Linn.), *Field Scabious.*

Scarce at Kierfiold — probably introduced (Dr Boswell).

ORDER XXVII.—COMPOSITÆ.

GENUS XCVI.—SOLIDAGO (Linn.)

193. S. VIRGAUREA, *Golden-rod.*

Local, but generally found where there are sandstone cliffs.   Hoy Hills, Holm, Orphir, and Fitty Hill are some of the localities.

Var. *Cambrica.*   On cliffs near Hobbister, Orphir.

GENUS XCVII.—BELLIS (Linn.)

194. B. PERENNIS (Linn.), *Daisy.*   Everywhere.

GENUS XCVIII.—ASTER.

195. A. TRIPOLIUM (Linn.), *Michaelmas Daisy.* Scarce.

Oyce, Firth; Copinshay; Quendale, Rousay, &c.

GENUS XCIX.— GNAPHALIUM.

196. G. ULIGINOSUM (Linn.), *Marsh Cudweed.* Common.

Var. *pilulare* (Koch) = *G. pilulare* (Wahlenberg). From loch forming mill dam, Eday, September 1905. Found same var. near Established Church, Burray. Fruit differs from type, which is glabrous, whilst this is hairy.

197. G. SYLVATICUM (Linn.), *Highland Cudweed.* Common.

198. G. SUPINUM.

This is given in "New Botanist's Guide," and placed in "Florula Orcadensis" in "Journal of Botany" for 1864.

GENUS C.—ANTENNARIA (Gærtn.)

199. A. DIOICA (Gærtn.), *Cat's-foot.* Scarce. Swanbister, Deerness, Holm, &c.

GENUS CI.—ACHILLEA (Linn.)

200. A. MILLEFOLIUM (Linn.), *Milfoil.* Common..

This plant is known in Orkney as "meal-an'-folly," which is no doubt a corrupted form of the technical term. It is said to have been used at one time in making a decoction like tea. The specimen in my herbarium is var. *lanata.* Neil says, "At a cottage door in Kirbuster, Deerness, a large collection of the flowering tops of the dwarfy milfoil was laid out to dry. They infuse this and drink it as tea. It is in repute for dispelling melancholy."

201. A. PTARMICA (Linn.), *Sneeze-wort.* Common. Sometimes this plant produces a deformed flower slightly resembling an unripe strawberry. It is probably produced by a gall.

GENUS CII.—ANTHEMIS (Mich.)

202. A. COTULA (Linn.), *Stinking Chamomile.*

Naturalised in Orphir; South Winbreck, Deerness; probably an escape.

203. A. NOBILIS (Linn.), *Common Chamomile.*

Met with very occasionally; near roadside, Rennibister (July 1883, Dr Fortescue) ; Winbreck, Deerness; no doubt introduced.

204. A. ARVENSIS (Linn.), *Corn Chamomile.*

Found in fields in Deerness (1894) ; Greentoft, Deerness (1906).

GENUS CIII.—CHRYSANTHEMUM (Linn.)

205. C. SEGETUM (Linn.), *Corn Marigold.* Common.

Strange to say, this is an exceedingly rare flower in Deerness, although in some parishes, as Birsay, it is one of the most abundant weeds.

206. C. LEUCANTHEMUM (Linn.), *Ox-eye Daisy.*

This flower is scarce. It is often found in churchyards, *e.g.,* Shapinsay, Holm, and on a mound of Campstone, St. Andrews, known as St. Peter's Church; probably not native.

207. C. PYRETHRUM (Syme).

Found in H. C. Watson's list as one of the plants reported by Syme in Orkney, but not in Dr Fortescue's.

GENUS CIV.—MATRICARIA (Linn.)

208. M. INODORA (Linn.), *Scentless Mayweed.* Common.

Var. *salina* (Bab.) This variety is met with more frequently than the species.

209. M. MARITIMA (Linn.), *Scentless Mayweed.*

A seashore plant which is not uncommon in Deerness, and no doubt found elsewhere. I sent roots for cultivation to Mr Hunnybun, Huntingdon. He says, "One of the plants you sent me is evidently *matricaria maritima.*" I gathered a few plants of *inodora* in Fair Isle, which I take to be *maritima*, but the ligules are yellow.

210. M. CHAMOMILLA (Linn.), *Wild Chamomile.*

This plant is probably introduced, but several escapes have become naturalised. Found it growing abundantly in a sheltered hollow in Beaquoy, Birsay.

GENUS CV.—TANACETUM (Linn.)

211. T. VULGARE (Linn.), *Tansy.*

Introduced, but now found frequently in yards and about farm houses, and used medicinally.

GENUS CVI.—ARTEMISIA (Linn.)

212. A. VULGARIS (Linn.), *Mugwort.*

This is a fairly common weed on the boundary line between fields. It is known in Orkney as "bulwands," in East Mainland as "grobbie." The tops of this plant were formerly used instead of hops for flavouring ale.

GENUS CVII.—TUSSILAGO (Linn.)

213. T. FARFARA (Linn.), *Colt's-foot.* Common.

A most difficult weed to eradicate when once established.

Genus CVIII.—PETASITES (Linn.)

214. P. VULGARIS, *Butter-bur.* Luckily scarce.

Extremely difficult to eradicate. Churchyards— Shapinsay and St. Andrews ; Burn of Aikersness, Evie ; Birsay, &c.

Genus CIX.—SENECIO (Linn.)

215. S. VULGARIS (Linn.), *Groundsel.* Common.

216. S. JACOBÆA (Linn.), *Ragwort.* Common on dry, sandy pastures.

Var. *flosculosus* (Jord.) This variety is frequently met with among the above. It seems to me there are several grades from this rayless variety to those with full rays.

217. S. VISCOSUS (Linn.), *Stinking Groundsel.*

This plant was reported by Dr Clouston. It may have been a mistake for *sylvaticus.* Not since met with as far as I know.

218. S. SYLVATICUS (Linn.), *Mountain Groundsel.* Very rare.

Found it on barn of Bigging, Birsay ; and among whins above Established Church, St. Andrews (M. Spence) ; Smogrow, Orphir (Dr Boswell). Dr Fortescue says, " It seems to have disappeared at the last place.

219. S. AQUATICUS (Huds.), *Marsh Ragwort.* Common.

These are called " tirsics " in East Mainland, " tirsoos " in West Mainland.

GENUS CX.—INULA (Linn.)

220. I. HELENIUM (Linn.), *Elecampane.*

This is no doubt a plant which has been introduced for medicinal purposes. It is one of a small group often found in kale-yards.

GENUS CXI.—CNICUS (Linn.)

221. C. LANCEOLATUS (Willd.), *Spear Thistle.* Common.

222. C. PALUSTRIS (Willd.), *Marsh Thistle.* Common.

223. C. ARVENSIS (Hoffm.), *Creeping Thistle.* Common.

Some of these are white beneath the leaves and densely tomotose, which seems to be Buchanan Whyte's variety *argenteus.* In Hooker's "Flora," 3rd edition (Students'), var. *setosus* (Bess.) is given as growing in Orkney. Dr Fortescue writes :—" In 'English Botany' the following occurs :—' Var. *setosus* not native, but found about Culross, not far from Dunfermline ; it has also been found about Battersea, Hartlepool, and at Kirkwall, Orkney.' I have specimens of this plant from England, and could not have overlooked it had I met with it in Orkney. I looked at every patch of *arvensis* which I saw in Orkney with the hope of meeting with it, but never did so. I think my uncle (Dr Boswell) said it had been found between Kirkwall and Finstown. It may have been introduced and afterwards died out."

GENUS CXII.—ARCTIUM (Linn.), *Burdock*.

224. A. INTERMEDIUM (Lange).

This plant is found on links and waste places —Newark, Deerness ; Hoy, Westray, &c. In Dr Duguid and R. Heddle's list *nemorosum* is given ; but, as some doubt regarding its accuracy had been expressed, I sent my specimen from Newark to Mr Ar. Bennett, who said it was as above, with this reservation—that the specimen was not a whole plant. In "Ann. Scot. Nat. Hist.," July 1895, Col. H. H. Johnston, C.B., states that specimens from Hoy were identified by the late Dr T. J. B. Boswell on the authority of Prof. C. C. Babington. Specimens from Skaill were identified by Prof. Babington as probably *A. nemorosum* (Lej.)

GENUS CXIII.—SAUSSUREA.

225. S. ALPINA (DC.), *Alpine saussurea*. Rather scarce.

Hoy Hills (Dr Boswell). I received a few fine specimens from Rousay (Kierfiold Hill) through Mr McKay, Schoolhouse, Finstown.

GENUS XIV —CENTAUREA (Linn.), *Knap-weed*.

226. C. NIGRA (Linn.)

This plant is met with occasionally—Wideford brae, Dingeshowe, Westray, &c. ; fairly common in Sanday and Burray.

227. C. CYANUS (Linn.), *Corn Bluebottle*.

Stray plants occur here and there among oats. I don't think, however, it is a native. It is found in Caithness.

Genus CXV.—LAPSANA (Linn.), *Nipplewort.*

228. L. communis (Linn.). Not common.

Genus CXVI.—CICHORIUM (Linn.), *Chicory.*

229. C. Intybus (Linn.)

Several farmers are sowing this among grasses for pasture.

Genus CXVII.—CREPIS (Linn.)

230. C. capellaris (Wallr.), *Hawksbeard.*

In several fields in Deerness and St. Andrews; Grainbank (Dr Flett); no doubt elsewhere.

231. C. biennis (Linn.)

A few plants were found in grass fields—introduced. My specimens from Quoybelloch, Deerness.

Genus CXVIII.—HIERACIUM (Linn.)

232. H. Pilosella (Linn.), *Mouse-eared Hawkweed.*

Hoy, Firth, St. Andrews, Rousay. Scarce, but found in several dry localities.

233. H. iricum (Fr.), *Alpine Hawkweed.*

Hoy Hill, Pegal Burn (Dr Boswell); Wart Hill, Rousay (July 1907, M. Spence).

234. H. Schmidtii (Tausch), *Hawkweed.*

Var. *crinigerum* (Fries.) Hoy (July 1883, Col. H. H. Johnston, C.B.) (See *H. vulgatum* (Fries.) in "Scot. Nat.," No. XLVIII., Oct. 1882, p. 370.)

235. H. orcadense (W. R. Linton).

This species is given in the 10th edition of "London

Catalogue," and is said to have been found in no other county. Professor Babington gives cliffs, Hoy, as the locality.

236. H. SCOTICUM (F. J. Hanb.), *Hawkweed.* Very rare.

On cliffs at seashore, Hangaback, Gyre, Orphir (Aug. 1885, Col. H. H. Johnston, C.B.)

237. H. BRITANNICUM (F. J. Hanb.), *Hawkweed.*
Crags on hillside, Dwarfie Hammers, Hoy (Aug 1883, Col. H. H. Johnston, C.B.)

238. H. CORYMBOSUM (Fries.), *Hawkweed.*
Var. *salicifolium.* Cliffs at seashore, Hobbister, Orphir (Aug. 1880, Col. H. H. Johnston, C.B.)

239. H. STRICTUM (Fries.), *Hawkweed.*
Var. *amplidentatum* (F. J. Hanbury). Pegal Bay, Walls, Hoy (collected by Miss J. B. Irvine Fortescue in Aug. 1880.)

240. H. VULGATUM (Fries.)
Hoy Hill; Waulk Mill Bay and Hobbister (Dr Boswell). The last two are considered to be the same plant by some botanists.

241. H. AURATUM (Fries.), *Hawkweed.*
Sandstone cliffs at the seashore, south side of Pegal Bay, Walls, Hoy (Aug. 1894, Col. H. H. Johnston, C.B.)

242. H. ANGLICUM (Fries.), *Hawkweed.*

Hoy Hill ; Scapa ; Hobbister (Dr Boswell) ; Wart Hill, Rousay (M. Spence).

243. H. MURORUM (Linn.), *Hawkweed.*

Hoy Hill (Dr Boswell) ; Scapa ; Gaitnip.

244. H. PULCHELLUM, *Hawkweed.*

Wart Hill, Rousay (July 1907, M. Spence).

245. H. CAESIUM (Fries.)

Speeimens from Hoy Hill, collected in 1849, are named as above by Mr James Backhouse. Dr Boswell thinks they are *H. murorum.*

GENUS CXIX.—HYPOCHŒRIS (Linn.)

246. H. RADICATA (Linn.), *Cat's Ear.* Common.

GENUS CXX.—LEONTODON (Linn.)

247. L. AUTUMNALIS (Linn.), *Hawkbit.* Common.

Var. *praetensis* (Koch). The more common form. Var. *simplex* (Dub.) found near top of Ward Hill, Orphir, 12th Aug. 1908. Leaves were entire ; only one flower. Mr Ar. Bennett saw specimen.

GENUS CXXI. –TARAXACUM (Hall).

248. T. OFFICINALE (Weber), *Dandelion.* Common.

249. T. ERYTHROSPERUM (Andrz.) Fairly common.

250. T. PALUSTRE (DC.)

I found this in meadow west of Stembister, St. Andrews—the only locality in which I have seen it.

251. T. UDUM (Jord.)

Roadside, Gyre, Orphir (Oct. 1880, Col. H. H. Johnston, C.B.); grassy banks, Hoy (July 1877, Col. H. H. Johnston, C.B.)

GENUS CXXII.—SONCHUS (Linn.)

252. S. OLERACEUS (Linn.), *Sowthistle*. Scarce.
Have seldom found it; North Sands, Deerness (1900).

253. S. ASPER (Hoffm.), *Sowthistle*.
This plant is fairly common.

254. S. ARVENSIS (Linn.), *Corn Sowthistle*. Common.

ORDER XXVIII.—CAMPANULACEÆ.

GENUS CXXIII.—LOBELIA (Linn.)

255. L. DORTMANNA (Linn.), *Water Lobelia*. Very rare.

Landswater, Walls; Rousay (R. Heddle). This may at some time have been introduced, as it is considered a suitable plant for cultivating in trout-fishing lochs. In fact, the factor some years ago spoke of introducing the plant into the two hill lochs, Walls, without knowing that it had been there for many years.

GENUS CXXIV.—JASIONE (Linn.)

256. J. MONTANA (Linn.), *Sheep's Scabious*.

Confined to Eday and North Ronaldshay. The meadow near the South Lighthouse in Fair Isle was covered with this plant in July 1894. Sepals hairy, peduncles hirsute. After pointing out to Mr Ar.

Bennett that this plant differs somewhat from those described in my botany books, he wrote : —" Four of my 'English Floras' insist on *glabrous peduncles*. Two or three Continentals do not do this. So your plant differs from the ordinary plant by having, first, hispid peduncles ; second, hispid calyx lobes.

ORDER XXIX.—ERICACEÆ.

GENUS CXXV.—ARCTOSTAPHYLOS (Adans.)

257. A. ALPINA (Spreng.), *Bear-berry*. Scarce. Hills, Hoy and Rousay.

258. A. UVA-URSI (Spreng.), *Red Bear-berry*. Rare. Hoy Hills and Walls.

GENUS CXXVI.—CALLUNA (Salisb.)

259. C. VULGARIS (Sal.), *Common Ling*.

Var. *glabrata* is found on nearly all the islands. A hairy variety occurs near the Berry, Walls (Dr Fortescue).

GENUS CXXVII.—ERICA (Linn.)

260. E. TETRALIX (Linn.), *Cross-leaved Heath*. Common.

261. E. CINEREA (Linn.), *Fine-Leaved Heath*. Common.

GENUS CXXVIII.—LOISELEURIA (Desv.), *Azalea*.

262. L. PROCUMBENS. Very rare.

Hoy Hills and Knap of Trowie Glen, Hoy (Dr Boswell).

GENUS CXXIX.—PYROLA (Linn.)

263. P. ROTUNDIFOLIA (Linn.), *Winter-green.*

In the valley near the Little Water, Rousay, to
the right of a burn flowing towards Sourin, among
the gouks near the foot of the hill. There was a
beautiful display in July 1907, when I found it for the
(to me) first time. I have no accurate information as
to its being found elsewhere. Received a plant from
Mr Omond, Orphir, which I believe was this. Flowers
were in bud. It was found in Orphir. Dr Fortescue
informs me he has a specimen from Rousay, but not
from near the small loch.

ORDER XXX.—VACCINIACEÆ.

GENUS CXXX.—VACCINIUM (Linn.)

264. V. VITIS-IDÆA (Linn.), *Red Cow-berry.* Scarce.
Hoy Hills ; Walls ; Rousay ; Orphir.

265. V. ULIGINOSUM (Linn.), *Great Bilberry.* Rare.
Walls ; Hoy Hill ; Birsay. *f. rotundata* is a
variety that J. Spence, Overabist, Birsay, found near
Howally, in his district. There were only a few
clumps of it. I sent a specimen to Mr A. Bennett, who
says it differs from the common form by the greater
rotundity of its leaves. This is, as far as we know,
the first time this distinction has been noticed. Mr
Bennett says :—" I have never seen such shaped
leaves before. Your species puzzled me at first, for
the peduncles of the flowers are so short, but the
flower, shape, &c., are *uliginosum.* I have looked up

twenty 'Floras' and find no mention of a plant like yours."

266. V. MYRTILLUS (Linn.), *Blaeberry.* Common.

f. microphylla (Lange). Mr Bennett noticed this variety among some specimens sent him. I found it on top of Blotchnie Hill, Rousay, above Trumland. He informs me it also occurs on Saxa Vord Hill, in Shetland (18th Dec. 1907).

ORDER XXXI.—PRIMULACEÆ.

GENUS CXXXI.—PRIMULA (Linn.)

267. P. VULGARIS (Linn.), *Common Primrose.* Common.

268. P. VERIS (Linn.), *Cowslip.*

At Links of Aikerness (Dr Duguid and R. Heddle); cliffs between Hoy Head and Kame (Col. H. H. Johnston, C.B.) Dr Flett found this on Tuquoy Links, Westray, and gave me specimens.

Var. *intermedia* is given in Dr Fortescue's list as growing with *p. veris* on links, Aikerness, on authority of Dr Duguid and R. Heddle. This is probably the "*intermedia*" of Dr Hooker, given as a possible hybrid between *P. veris* and some other variety.

269. P. SCOTICA (Hook.), *Scottish Primrose.*

This beautiful little plant is found in several localities, but seems to be most abundant in Westray. It flowers in June and again in September. A few roots I planted in my garden bloomed one summer in May

July, and September after it had been under cultivation for three years. It is found at Black Craig,
Stromness, Standing Stones, Stenness ; in Rousay,
Walls, Shapinsay, and North Ronaldshay. It is also
abundant on links, Papa Westray. A few plants grow
near Biggings, St. Andrews. These and specimens
from Papa Westray differ in length of flower stalk, in
hairiness of capsule and shape of leaves. Mr Ar.
Bennett says:—" I can see the difference in the two
specimens of *Primula*. I can find no var. given of
P. scotica. It is of limited distribution. The floras
of Norway and Sweden give no varieties." One has
a much shorter, grooved flower stalk than the other ;
the other is longer and smoother. It has been
suggested by an eminent botanist that this variety
should be named *P. scotica* var. *orcadensis*. If,
under cultivation, it retains these characteristics, it
will be so named.

Genus CXXXII.—LYSIMACHIA.

270. L. NEMORUM (Linn.), *Yellow Pimpernel*.

Gills at Scapa; Swanbister Burn; Quoys Burn,
Hoy. In August 1912 I found a patch of these along
a path leading from Burn of Quoys to Dwarfie Stone.

Genus CXXXIII.—TRIENTALIS (Linn.)

271. T. EUROPÆA (Linn.), *Chickweed Wintergreen*.

Kingsdale, Firth. G. Robson, teacher, Birsay, so
the story goes, was surveying this hillside when he
came across this, till then, unknown plant in Orkney.
He was a keen botanist, and set such value on the
discovery that he threw down his chain and set out

for Kirkwall to consult Dr Duguid and R. Heddle. It is also found on the Orphir side of same hill. J. Omond, teacher, Kirbuster, got a plant here. These are the only known habitats of the plant in Orkney. Wm. McKay, teacher, Finstown, gave me specimens. Naversdale, Orphir (Dr Fortescue, July 1889).

GENUS CXXXIV.—GLAUX (Linn.)

272. G. MARITIMA (Linn.), *Sea Milkwort.*

Fairly common along gravelly seashore.

GENUS CXXXV.—ANAGALLIS (Linn.)

273. A. ARVENSIS (Linn.), *Poor Man's Weather-glass.*

Fields at Westness, Rousay (R. Heddle); field below Booth, Deerness (September 1895, M. Spence). No doubt brought with farm seeds in both cases.

274. A. TENELLA (Linn.), *Bog Pimpernel.* Not uncommon.

This plant is described in Hooker as glabrous, but there is a variety in Orkney with glandular sepals and capsule; first noticed by Dr Grant.

ORDER XXXII.—GENTIANACEÆ.

GENUS CXXXVI.—GENTIANA (Linn.)

275. G. CAMPESTRIS (Linn.), *Gentian.* Common.

276. G. BALTICA (Murb.), *Dwarf Gentian.* Very rare.

North Ronaldshay and top of cliffs, Swanney,

Birsay.　Mr Ar. Bennett says of it :—" Yes, the dwarf *gentian* was odd ; yet I could make nothing of it.　At first I thought you had found *G. succica*, but it would not fit in."　Specimens were again sent from Swanney in September 1912.　These, he said were *G. baltica* (Murb.), a sub-species of *campestris*.　As this is given in latest edition of " London Catalogue " as a species, I so enter it here.　Probably this is the plant recorded by Dr Wallace in 1700, and designated *Gentiana autumnalis*.

277. G. AMARELLA (Linn.), *Small-flowered Gentian.*

Links, Aikerness ; Deerness ; Hoxa, &c.

GENUS CXXXVII.—MENYANTHES (Linn.), *Buckbean.*

278. M. TRIFOLIATA (Linn.)　Fairly common in boggy places.

ORDER XXXIII.—CONVOLVULACEÆ.

GENUS CXXXVIII.—CONVOLVULUS (Linn.)

279. C. ARVENSIS (Linn.), *Bindweed.*

I have never seen this except in gardens and their immediate vicinity.

ORDER XXXIV.—SCROPHULARIACEÆ.

GENUS CXXXIX.—SCROPHULARIA (Linn.)

280. S. NODOSA (Linn.), *Knotted Figwort.*

Burn of Redland, Firth ; and burn above church, Firth (Dr Duguid).　I have looked for but been unable to get it in either place.

GENUS CXL.—DIGITALIS (Linn.)

281. D. PURPUREA (Linn.), *Foxglove.*

Fairly common on the heaths, where shelter is obtained; in Hoy and the East and West Mainland.

GENUS CXLI.—VERONICA (Linn.)

282. V.HEDERÆFOLIA (Linn.), *Ivy-leaved Speedwell.* Common.

283. V. POLITA (Fries.), *Field Speedwell.* Fairly common.

Swanbister, Houton (Dr Boswell); Hobbister (R. Heddle); Hurteso, Holm (M. Spence).

284. V.AGRESTIS(Linn.),*Field Speedwell.* Common.

285. V. ARVENSIS(Linn.), *Wall Speedwell.* Common. Var. *eximia* (Townsend). Fields, Deerness.

286. V.SERPYLLIFOLIA (Linn.), *Thyme-leaved Speed-well.* Common.

Var. *humifusa* (Dickson). Deerness and St. Andrews (M. Spence).

287. V. OFFICINALIS (Linn.), *Common Speedwell.* Common.

288. V. CHAMÆDRYS (Linn.), *Germander Speedwell.*

Corner of field in which E.C. Manse, Holm, stands. I could not find it here, but got it near the farm steading, Turmiston, Stenness (Oct. 1895); and Mr Omond, Orphir, has found several in Kirbuster, Orphir (1903), and sent me specimens. I have specimens also from

Rousay. Dr Fortescue says:—"Now established at Swanbister and Binscarth, where it was introduced by Miss Bain, along with other British wild flowers not indigenous to Orkney."

289. V. SCUTELLATA (Linn.), *Marsh Speedwell.*

Local, but found in many parishes—Deerness, St. Andrews, &c.

290. V. BUXBAUMII (Ten.), *Field Speedwell.*

Found several plants in field of Crea and Booth, Deerness (Aug. 1906) ; on farm of Stove, Sanday (Sept. 1909, M. Spence).

291. V. ANAGALLIS-AQUATICA (Linn.), *Water Speedwell.*

Local, but in several parishes — Deerness, St. Andrews, Evie, &c.

292. V. BECCABUNGA (Linn.), *Brooklime.*

Local, but often met with in water-courses and ditches—Deerness, St. Andrews, &c.

GENUS CXLII.—EUPHRASIA (Linn.)

293. E. OFFICINALIS (Linn.), *Eyebright.* Common.

Var. *Rostkoviana* (Hayne) ; common. Var. *gracilis* (Fries.) ; common. Var. *maritima* (Hook.) ; Mull Head, Deerness.

GENUS CXLIII.—BARTSIA (Linn.)

294. B. ODONTITES (Huds.), *Red Bartsia.* Scarce.

Var. *verna* (Reichb). Local, but to be found in most parishes of Mainland—Deerness, Holm, Orphir, St. Andrews, &c.

Genus CXLIV.—PEDICULARIS (Linn.), *Marsh Lousewort.*

295. P. palustris (Linn.) Common.

296. P. sylvatica (Linn.), *Field Lousewort.* Common.

Genus CXLV.—RHINANTHUS (Linn.)

297. R. Crista-galli (Linn.), *Yellow Rattle.* Common.

298. R. major (Ehrh.), *Yellow Rattle.*

Var. *stenopterus* (Fries.) This has been a frequent weed of cultivation on farms of Newark and Quoybelloch, Deerness, for several years. It was probably introduced with seeds, but has established itself for some years. Dr Fortescue saw it in fields between Lingro and Greenigoe in 1890.

Genus CXLVI.—MELAMPYRUM (Linn.)

299. M. pratense (Linn.), *Cow-wheat.* Not common. Naversdale ; Hoy ; Ward Hill, Orphir.

Var. *montanum* (Johnst.) Naversdale and Berriedale, Hoy (Dr Boswell).

300. M. sylvaticum (Linn.), *Wood Cow-wheat.* Pastures (R. Heddle).

Order XXXV.—LABIATÆ.

Genus CXLVII.—MENTHA (Linn.), *Mint.*

301. M. aquatica (Linn.)

Var. *hirsuta* (Huds.) Common in marshes.

302. M. ARVENSIS (Linn.), *Corn Mint.* Rare.

It is given in R. Heddle's list of plants as local. I have never met with it where it seemed to be native.

303. M. PIPERITA (Linn.), *Peppermint.* Rare.

In September 1911 I found a considerable patch in a marsh near the source of the burn passing the Public School, St. Andrews. The burn leading into this marsh passes, I think, only one small croft occupied by Pratt. It is not likely to have come from there. I am inclined to consider it native, especially in view of subsequent finds. Also found in East Ross, Banff and Aberdeen, but not considered native in last two. Found several in burn above Quoykay, St. Andrews, in 1912.

GENUS CXLVIII.—NEPETA (Linn.)

304. N. HEDERACEA (Trev.), *Ground Ivy.* Not common.

This plant is established in several places, but always seems to be a garden escape. Used formerly for medicinal purposes.

GENUS CXLIX.—THYMUS (Linn.), *Thyme.*

305. T. SERPYLLUM (Linn.)

This is a common plant in the West Mainland. I have never seen it in Deerness, nor, I think, in any other part of the East Mainland.

GENUS CL.—PRUNELLA (Linn.)

306. P. VULGARIS (Linn.), *Self-heal.* Common.

I have sometimes met with a white variety, with

pale green leaves. Its appearance is different, but in detail there is little difference.

Genus CLI.—SCUTELLARIA.

307. S. galericulata (Linn.), *Skull-cap.*

This plant is found only in North Ronaldshay. Rev. W. McPherson first told me of it. Mr Scott, Old Manse, sent me specimens in August 1910.

Genus CLII.—STACHYS (Linn.)

308. S. palustris (Linn.), *Marsh-woundwort.* Common.

Var. *S. ambigua* (Sm.) Common. *Palustris* is sometimes so felted on both sides as to be var. *canescens* (Lange).

309. S. sylvatica (Linn.), *Hedge-woundwort.* Rare.

Houton (Dr Boswell) ; near churchyard (Holm) ; Redland, Firth (M. Spence).

310. S. arvensis (Linn.), *Corn-woundwort.* Rare. This is reported from fields, Rackwick. I found fine specimens in a field of turnips on the farm of Quoyer, Birsay. Mr Bennett says they are the largest he had ever seen.

Genus CLIII.—GALEOPSIS (Linn.)

311. G. versicolor (Curt.), *Hemp-nettle.* Cornfields, Orphir ; Westness, &c. (R. Heddle).

312. G. Tetrahit (Linn.), *Common Hemp-nettle.* Common.

Var. *bifida* (Boenn.) Common (Dr Boswell).

GENUS CLIV.—LAMIUM (Linn.), *Dead-nettle.*

313. L. AMPLEXICAULE (Linn.), *Henbit Dead-nettle.* Common.

314. L. INTERMEDIUM (Fries.) Common.

315. L. HYBRIDUM (Vill.)

In fields (Messrs Heddle and Duguid).

316. L. PURPUREUM (Linn.), *Red Dead-nettle.* Common.

317. L. ALBUM, (Linn.), *White Dead-nettle.*

Low reported this plant in his flora of the county. It was lost sight of till 1895, when I found it near the steading of the glebe of the Established Church Manse, Holm.

GENUS CLV.—AJUGA (Linn.), *Bugle.*

318. A. REPTANS (Linn.), *Common Bugle.* Fairly common.

Rousay, Firth, Holm, &c.

319. A. PYRAMIDALIS (Linn.), *Pyramidal Bugle.* Rare.

Sides of hill on right hand from Berriedale to Rackwick (Dr Duguid) ; since at Rackwick (R. Heddle) ; Naversdale, Orphir, In considerable quantity, Hill of Hoy (1849, Dr Boswell) ; also Berriedale. (See " Bot. Gazette," Vol. II., p. 107, 1850.)

GENUS CLVI.—TEUCRIUM (Linn.)

320. T. SCORODONIA (Linn.), *Wood-sage.* Not often met with.

Banks of Oyce, Firth ; Crook, Orphir ; Berstane ; Gill Burn ; Naversdale ; Hoy.

ORDER XXXVI.—BORAGINACEÆ.

GENUS CLVII.—ECHIUM (Linn.)

321. E. VULGARE (Linn.), *Viper's Bugloss.*

Found in cornfields—no doubt an escape. Flaws, Holm; Skelbister, Orphir; Lopness, Sanday.

GENUS CLVIII.—SYMPHYTUM (Linn.)

322. S. OFFICINALE (Linn.), *Comfrey.*

Var. *patens* (Sibth.) Found in Hoy by Dr Grant, but he thinks introduced. It is growing as a weed in garden of Bu, Burray—introduced.

GENUS CLIX.—MERTENSIA, (Roth.)

323. M. MARITIMA (Gray), *Oyster Plant.*

This is one of our prettiest plants, and fairly abundant on several shores. It grows freely just above high-water mark, on the seaweed cast up by the sea. It is found in Holm, Deerness, South Ronaldshay, Sanday, Walls, Birsay, &c.

GENUS CLX.—LYCOPSIS (Linn.)

324. L. ARVENSIS (Linn.), *Bugloss.* Fairly common, but local.

It is found generally in sandy soils—Deerness, Houton, Aikerness, &c.

GENUS CLXI.—MYOSOTIS (Linn.), *Scorpion Grass.*

325. M. CÆSPITOSA (Schultz). Common in rills and burns.

326. M. ARVENSIS (Hill), *Field Scorpion-grass.* Common.

327. M. PALUSTRIS (With.), *Water Forget-me-not.* Rare.

My specimen was found in ditch on farm of Hall of Tankerness. Plants found in burn, Swanbister, are said to be escapes. I have no reason to think my plant is other than native.

Var. *strigulosa.* Rare. Scapa (Dr Boswell).

328. M. REPENS (Don), *Creeping Forget-me-not.* Rare.

Swanbister; Papdale (Dr Boswell).

329. M. VERSICOLOR (Sm.), *Forget-me-not.* Common.

330. M. COLLINA (Hoffm.), *Early Forget-me-not.* Not common.

I have gathered it a few times only, in grass fields.

ORDER XXXVII.—LENTIBULARIACEÆ.

GENUS CLXII.—PINGUICULA (Linn.), *Butterwort*

331. P. VULGARIS (Linn.). Common in bogs. Orkney name—*Eccle-grass.*

332. P. LUSITANICA (Linn.), *Pale Butterwort.*

Dr Fortescue found this once at Westquoys, Orphir. Low has it in his " Flora." I do not have a specimen. Dr Fortescue says :—" I once stumbled on a few plants of this when walking from the west end of the Loch of Kirbuster, in Orphir, to Swanbister. It was growing on wet, bare patches of peat among tufts of heather on flat, boggy grounds on the property of Westquoys, some 200 yards from the Orphir-Stenness road.

Genus CLXIII.—UTRICULARIA (Linn.)

333. U. MINOR (Linn.), *Smaller Bladderwort.*

Dr Flett found this above Orphir road, near bridge to east of Scapa School. It grows abundantly in a large depression—probably old quarries—on Harray side of public road after passing dykes of Binscarth for Birsay.

ORDER XXXVIII.—PLUMBAGINACEÆ.

Genus CLXIV.—STATICE (Linn.)

334. S. MARITIMA (Mill.), *Sea-pink.* Common.

My specimens, gathered on Deerness shore, have three veined leaves and pubescent scapes. No doubt they are var. *planifolia* (Syme). The thick tuberous roots of *Statice maritima* were formerly sliced and boiled with milk for human consumption.

ORDER XXXIX.—PLANTAGINACEÆ.

Genus CLXV.—PLANTAGO (Linn.), *Plantain.*

335. P. MAJOR (Linn.) Common.

336. P. MARITIMA (Linn.) Common.

Var. *minor* (Hooker, " Brit. Flora," 1830, p. 67). Leaves linear, lanceolate, densely hairy, as well as the scape, which is the same as var. *hirsuta* (Syme). Var. *hirsuta* (Syme) is given as a species in Edmondston's " Flora of Shetland," 2nd edit., 1903. It is given as found near house of Skaill by Hooker; at Baltasound by Beeby (" Scot. Nat. Hist.," 1887.) Dr Grant gathered several specimens in the neighbourhood of Black Craig in August 1912. This species—or, more correctly, variety—is found only in Orkney and Shetland. Dr Fortescue writes :—"A remarkable hairy form, with short and fleshy leaves, grows on the cliffs south-west of the Kame of Hoy ; Ward Hill, Hoy (Aug. 1886) ; pastures, Ramnigoe (July 1886, Col. H. H. Johnston. C.B.) Var. *hirsuta* (Syme) is more plentiful in Shetland. Var. *linearis* (Syme, in " Eng. Botany") is the antithesis of the very hairy form *hirsuta*, and is common on sea-washed grassy shores.

337. P. LANCEOLATA (Linn.,) *Ribwort*. Common.

Some of the larger plants in Orkney have seven veins in their leaves instead of five. To these Syme gave the designation var. *major*.

338. P. CORONOPUS (Linn.), *Buck's-horn Plantain*. Common.

GENUS CLXVI.—LITTORELLA (Linn.)

339. L. LACUSTRIS (Linn.), *Shore-weed*. Common.

ORDER XL.—CHENOPODIACEÆ.

GENUS CLXVII.—SUÆDA (Forsk.)

340. S. MARITIMA (Dum.), *Sea-blite*. Scarce.

Fidge, Swanbister ; Bay of Woodwick ; Mill, Sebay, St Andrews ; shore near mill, Tankerness, &c.

GENUS CLXVIII.—SALSOLA (Linn.)

341. S. KALI (Linn.), *Saltwort*. Very rare.

I found this above high-water mark at Newark

Bay (1896). It then disappeared till 1905, when two or three plants re-appeared. It has not been seen since.

GENUS CLXIX.—SALICORNIA (Linn.), *Glasswort*.

342. S. HERBACEA (Linn.)

Fidge, Swanbister; Peerie Sea; Oyce, Firth.

Var. *S. procumbens* (Sm.) Below mill, Sebay (M. Spence).

GENUS CLXX.—CHENOPODIUM (Linn.), *Goose-foot*.

343. C. ALBUM (Linn.) Scarce.

Swanbister; Bay of Woodwick; Hoy—farm east of manse.

GENUS CLXXI.—ATRIPLEX.

344. A. AUGUSTIFOLIA (Sm.)

Stenness (Dr Boswell).

345. A. ERECTA (Huds.) Fairly common.

Fidge, Swanbister; Sebay. *Angustifolia* and *erecta* are generally included as varieties under one species—*A. patula*.

346. A. BABINGTONII (Woods.) Common.

Var. *rosea* (Bab.) Fairly common.

347. A. LACINIATA (Linn.)

I once sent a young plant from the shore of Sebay to Mr Ar. Bennett, which he considered was this. P. Neil recorded it as common on sea-shores.

Order XLI.—POLYGONACEÆ.

Genus CLXXII.—RUMEX (Linn.), *Dock.*

348. R. OBTUSIFOLIUS (Linn.)   Common.

349. R. ACUTUS (Linn.), *Meadow Dock.*   Scarce.

Gritley, Deerness; Crantit; St. Andrews, &c. This is generally thought to be a hybrid of *R. obtusifolius* and *R. crispus* (Dr Boswell 1873).

350. R. CRISPUS (Linn.), *Curled Dock.*   Common.

Var. *triangulatus* (Syme).   Fairly common.

Var. *subcordatus* (Warr.)   Stembister (Sept. 1908, M. Spence).

351. R. AQUATICUS (Linn.), *Water Dock.*   Fairly Common.

352. R. SANGUINEUS (Linn.), *Bloody-veined Dock.*

I have specimens sent me by J. Spence, Overabist, Hillside, Birsay.   It was also reported by Neill in 1888.

353. R. ACETOSELLA (Linn.), *Sheep's Sorrel.* Common.

Var. *angiocarpus* (Murb.)   This is also found.

354. R. ACETOSA (Linn.), *Sorrel.*   Common.

Genus CLXXIII.—OXYRIA (Hill).

355. O. RENIFORMIS (Hook.), *Mountain Sorrel.* Not common; Hoy Hills.

Genus CLXXIV.—POLYGONUM (Linn.)

356. P. Convolvulus (Linn.), *Black Bindweed.*
Scarce.

Nether Scapa; fields in Harray (Prof. Trail); farm of Quoyer, Birsay (Sept. 1905, M. Spence).

357. P. aviculare (Linn.), *Knot-grass.* Common.
    (a) agrestinum (Jord.)
    (b) vulgatum (Syme).
    (c) microspermum (Jord.)
    (d) litorale (Link.)

(a) (b) and (c) are given in Dr Fortescue's list; (d) is a form sometimes met with on the sandy shore.

358. P. Persicaria (Linn.), *Spotted Knot-grass.*
Fairly common.

In wet patches in many fields on the Mainland, at least; Harray and Birsay (Prof. J. W. H. Trail).

359. P. lapathifolium (Linn.), *Pale Knot-grass.*
Scarce.

Skail, Westray (Dr Flett); Swanbister—introduced (Dr Boswell).

360. P. amphibium (Linn.), *Amphibious Bistort.*
Fairly common.

Var. *aquaticum.* In several places—Birsay, North Ronaldshay; Loch of Housby, Birsay, &c.

Var. *terrestre.* In several places—Deerness, Birsay, &c.; Crantit (July 1876); Loch of Brue, Lady, Sanday (July 1883, Col. H. H. Johnston, C.B.); Bridge of Brodgar; Skail (Dr Boswell).

361. P. BISTORTA (Linn.), *Snake-weed.*

In summer of 1911 J. Omond, Orphir, sent one he had found outside the garden of Swanbister. J. Firth, Finstown, gave me a plant he had found in a field in Firth. These are probably escapes. It is also given by P. Neil.

362. P. VIVIPARUM (Linn.), *Alpine Bistort.* Local and scarce.

West side of Rousay; Egilshay (Dr Duguid); side of hill above peat bog, Shapinsay (Wm McKay). It is more abundant on the hill-side above Pierowall, Westray, than any other place I know.

ORDER XLII.—EMPETRACEÆ.

GENUS CLXXV.—EMPETRUM (Linn.), *Crowberry.*

363. E. NIGRUM, (Linn.), *Blackberry.* Common on all the hills.

Mr Patrick Neil says:—" In Deerness we saw very strong ropes made from the shoots of the crowberry heath." This practice is still continued.

ORDER XLIII.—EUPHORBIACEÆ.

GENUS CLXXVI.—EUPHORBIA (Linn.)

364. E. HELIOSCOPIA (Linn.), *Sun Spurge.* Fairly common.

365. E. PEPLUS (Linn.), *Purple Spurge.*

This is not a native, but grows so abundantly year after year as a weed in gardens—such as Daisybank, Kirkwall—that it deserves mention here.

GENUS CLXXVII.—MERCURIALIS (Linn.), *Mercury.*

366. M. PERENNIS (Linn.)

Recorded by Miss Boswell. Dr Fortescue thinks this is probably a mistake.

ORDER XLIV.—CERATOPHYLLACEÆ.

GENUS CLXXVIII.—CERATOPHYLLUM (Linn.)

367. C. DEMERSUM (Linn.), *Common Hornwort.*

Loch of Ayre; Kirbuster (R. Heddle). I have never found this plant.

ORDER XLV.—UTRICACEÆ.

GENUS CLXXIX.—URTICA (Linn.), *Nettle.*

368. U. URENS, *Small Nettle.* Common.

369. U. DIOICA, *Great Nettle.* Common.

ORDER XLVI.—CUPULIFERÆ.

GENUS CLXXX.—CORYLUS (Linn.), *Hazel.*

370. C. AVELLANA (Linn.)

Berriedale and elsewhere in Hoy.

GENUS LXXXI.—BETULA (Linn.)

371. B. ALBA (Linn.), *Common Birch.*

In several places in Hoy (Dr Boswell); my specimens are from Hoy (2nd July 1902).

F

ORDER XLVII.—MYRICACEÆ.

Genus CLXXXII.—MYRICA (Linn.)

372. M. Gale (Linn.), *Sweet Gale.* Rare.

Eday (J. R. Hebden). I once found this plant on the meadows of Greeny, Birsay. It is also given in list of Dr Duguid and R. Heddle.

ORDER XLVIII.—SALICACEÆ.

Genus CLXXXIII.—POPULUS.

373. P. tremula (Linn.), *Aspen.*

Hoy; Walls; Hobbister, Orphir; cliffs on Calf of Flotta.

Genus CLXXXIV.—SALIX.

374. S. cinerea (Linn.), *Willow.* Rather scarce.

Var. *aquatica* (Sm.), Dr Boswell.

375. S. aurita (Linn.), *Round-eared Willow.* Common.

My specimens are from Wideford Burn and Hoy.

376. S. Caprea (Linn.), *Goat Willow.* Fairly common. Walls, Hoy, &c.

377. S. phylicifolia (Linn.), *Tea-leaved Willow.* Fairly common.

My specimens are from Walls and Redland. These larger salices—as the above four—are named *rice* in Orkney, from which several place-names are derived, as Ryssa, &c.

378. S. NIGRICANS (Sm.), *Dark-leaved Willow.*

One of the rarer salices; Groundwater, Orphir (Dr Boswell). I have a few specimens which Mr Ar. Bennett says are doubtful, but thinks they are *repens* × *nigricans.*

379. S. AMBIGUA (Ehrh.) Not common.

380. S. REPENS Linn., *(Dwarf Willow).*

Var. *fusca.* Common in sandy places (Dr Fortescue.) Two specimens I have are hybrids of *S. ambigua* and *S. repens* (Mr Ar. Bennett).

Var. *parvifolia* (Sm.), (Westray, 1905).

381. S. HERBACEA (Linn.), *Least Willow.*

I have specimens from Hoy (July 1902) which Mr Bennett says are the largest leaved specimens he ever saw. Neill, in his botanical tour through Orkney in 1804, reported *S. Lapponum, S. Arbuscula, S. Acuminata,* and *S. Angustifolia,* but no confirmation of these has been made either by Dr Fortescue or others.

382. S. RETICULATA (Linn.), *Reticulate Willow.*

This plant is given in Dr Fortescue's list as found in Hoy Hills by Mr Heddle.

383. S. MYRSINITES (Linn.), *Whortle-leaved Willow.*

Very rare. Hillside, Glen of Gair; Ward Hill, Hoy (July 1883, Col. H. H. Johnston, C.B., and Dr Fortescue). Dr Fortescue says :—" I believe this plant from Hoy has been taken as the type."

ORDER XLIX.—CONIFERÆ.

GENUS CLXXXV.—JUNIPERUS (Linn.)

384. J. COMMUNIS, *Juniper*.

Given in P. Neill's list; not in Dr Fortescue's. It is also given in "Florula Orcadensis" by H. C. Watson, F.L.S.

385. J. NANA (Willd.), *Juniper*.

Common in Hoy, Walls, Fair Isle. Dr Flett and I once found a plant on Ward Hill, Deerness. One plant at Swanbister, near Barmorie, in 1888 (Dr Fortescue). "The late Mr Johnston tells me (Dr Fortescue) that it used to grow near Lingro, by the side of the Orphir road."

Class II.—MONOCOTYLEDONES.

Order L.—TYPHACEÆ.

Genus CLXXXVI.—TYPHA (Linn.)

386. T. LATIFOLIA (Linn.), *Reed-mace.* Rare.

Loch of Aikerness—probably introduced. It occurs only in one patch covering about half-an-acre of the swamp, once a loch (Dr Fortescue).

Genus CLXXXVII.—SPARGANIUM (Linn.)

387. S. ERECTUM (Linn.), *Bur-reed.*

Local, but fairly common in some streams running into Loch Kirbuster; Cleenmar Burn, Orphir; Harray, Birsay, &c. My specimens were gathered near Græmeshall.

388. S. SIMPLEX (Huds.), *Bur-reed.*

Scapa Burn (Dr Duguid); Howan, Birsay (Prof. J. W. H. T. Trail).

389. S. AFFINE (Schnizl.), *Floating Bur-reed.* Rare.

Hoy (Syme); Standing Stones of Stenness (M. Spence); Sands Water, Walls; Lowrie's Water, Birsay; and Knitchin Loch, Rousay (G. Scarth).

b. microcephalum (Neum.) This variety grows in

one of the small lochs along the road from Hoy to Rackwick; Rev. E. S. Marshall found it. My specimens are from this. (See "Scottish Botanical Review," April 1912.)

ORDER LI.—LEMNACEÆ.

Genus CLXXXVIII.—LEMNA (Linn.)

390. L. MINOR (Linn.), *Duckweed.*

This plant was reported at first by Dr Macnab, but was subsequently considered doubtful. My specimens were gathered in bog below Ocilster, Holm. G. W. Scarth and I found it in a bog in Cross, Sanday. It is found on stagnant water.

ORDER LII.—NAIADACEÆ.

Genus CLXXXIX.—TRIGLOCHIN (Linn.), *Arrow-grass.*

391. T. PALUSTRE (Linn.), *Marsh Arrow-grass.* Common.

392. T. MARITIMUM (Linn.), *Seaside Arrow-grass.* Common on salt marshes.

Genus CXC.—POTAMOGETON (Linn.), *Pond-weed*

393. P. NATANS (Linn.), *Broad-leaved Pond-weed.* Fairly common.

Near Maeshowe and Loch of Harray (Dr Boswell). My specimens are from Flotta, in Birsay. The Orkney plant has unusually long peduncles.

394. P. HETEROPHYLLUS (Schreb.), *Pond-weed.* Common.

Var. *terrestre* (Meyer). I think this var. was from bog, Stove, Deerness, but not certain. Seen by Mr Ar. Bennett.

395. P. PERFOLIATUS (Linn.), *Pond-weed*. Common.

396. P. POLYGONIFOLIUS (Pour.), *Broad-leaved Pond-weed*. Fairly common.

My specimen is from Loch of Airy, Stronsay.

Var. *lancifolius* (Asch. and Græbn.) is the prior name for the var. *ericetorum* (Syme) in "English Botany" (Mr A. Bennett). Found by me in October 1908.

397. P. NITENS (Weber), *Pond-weed*.

Lochs of Harray and Boardhouse (Dr Boswell); Kirbuster, Orphir (July 1896).

Var. *salicifolius* (Fries.) Kirbuster, Orphir (July 1896, M. Spence); named by Mr A. Bennett.

398. P. PRÆLONGUS (Wulf.), *Long-stalked Pond-weed*.

Loch, Tankerness (21st Sept. 1911, M. Spence). This plant had not been previously found in Orkney. It grows in Caithness and the Færoes, but has not been found in Shetland.

399. P. PUSILLUS (Linn.), *Small Pondweed*.

Kirbuster Loch (Dr Boswell); St. Mary's Loch, Holm (M. Spence).

Var. *Berchtoldi* (Fieber). Dr Grant found this very rare variety of *pusillus* near Stairwaddy, Stromness. My specimens were got 21st Sept. 1911.

400. P. CRISPUS (Linn.), *Curly Pond-weed.* Rare.

Rousay (R. Heddle); in ditch draining Loch of Aikerness, Evie (1882). I could not find it there some years later. It grows in great abundance in Loch of Bea, Sanday, where, in 1909, G. W. Scarth and I gathered specimens.

401. P. PECTINATUS (Linn.), *Pond-weed.* Local, but not rare.

There are fine specimens in Loch Stenness and Loch Harray. Birsay and Harray (Prof. Trail).

402. P. FILIFORMIS (Nolte), *Narrow-leaved Pond-weed.* Fairly common.

In Loch of St. Tredwall, Papa Westray; Harray, near Windywalls; Loch of Harray, Loch of Tankerness, &c.

403. P. FRIESII (Rupr.), *Pond-weed.* Rare.

G. W. Scarth found this in one of the lochs near Start Lighthouse, Sanday (12th Sept. 1909). Dr Boswell, Mr Ar. Bennett tells me, had previously reported this from Orkney.

404. P. LUCENS (Linn.), *Shining Pond-weed.* Rare.

Mucklewater, Rousay (July 1890, Dr Fortescue); Stromness (1910, Dr Grant). "Some of the leaves are from 10 to 11 inches long" (Dr Fortescue).

Dr Fortescue sent specimens of most of the Orcadian *potamogetons* to Mr Arthur Bennett, F.L.S., a botanist with an unrivalled knowledge of British *potamogetons*. The latter gave me permission to use these notes as far as they helped to elucidate this difficult class :—

P. filiformis (Nolte). From Bridge of Brodgar, Harray (1880). This approaches *P. fasiculatus.*

P. heterophyllus. Kirbuster Loch (1875, Dr Boswell). A form with broad, submerged leaves. This answers to a Swedish specimen of *P. intermedius.*

P. nitens. (Birsay, 1876, Prof. Trail.) This is a remarkable plant, but seems best placed under *nitens.* It has the stem much branched, with enlongated peduncles.

P. pusillus, var. *rigidus* (A. Bennett) is a var. from Orkney, as stated in Hooker's "Student's Flora," but the locality is not mentioned. It is, he says, rigid, fragile ; leaves rigid, 1½ to 2½ inches long, accuminate strongly, one nerved, with two fainter nerves in some of the leaves ; stipules long, acute ; penduncles 1 inch long ; spike ½ inch long ; fruit slightly smaller than in typical *pusillus,* and less keeled on the back.

A remarkable form of *pusillus* gathered by Prof. Trail from the Loch of Stenness (Aug. 1876). It has much the aspect of *P. rutilus* (Wolfg.), but differs by its enlongated internodes, broader leaves, stipules, and fruit.

P. rufescens and *P. prælongus* might occur. (I have since found the latter, but not the former.—M.S.)

Genus CXCI.—ZANNICHELLIA (Linn.)

405. Z. POLYCARPA (Nolte), *Horned Pond-weed.*

Var. *tenuissima* (Fr.) Kirbuster Loch ; mill pond, Swanbister. These localities are given by Dr Fortescue. G. W. Scarth and I found it in loch forming lower mill-dam, near Pierowall, Westray (Sept. 1909).

Genus CXCII.—RUPPIA (Linn.)

406. R. SPIRALIS (Hartm.), *Tassel Pond-weed.* Not common.

Bridge of Brodgar ; Nether Biggings, Stenness ; in bay below Standing Stones of Stenness.

407. R. ROSTELLATA (Koch.)

Fidge, Swanbister.

Var. *nana* (Syme). Rare ; has creeping stems buried in the mud ; Oyce of Firth. This plant, when found by Dr Boswell, was new to British flora. It is now found in several places in north of Scotland. It grows in considerable abundance below mill, Sebay ; and in Ross and western Sutherland (Ar. Bennett).

Genus CXCIII.—ZOSTERA (Linn.), *Grasswrack.*

408. Z. marina (Linn.) Fairly common.

This plant grows very abundantly in Deersound, a little below low-water mark. It is driven ashore during gales, when farmers use it for thatching and manure. The soft, black mud in which it grows is called " mallock" in Deerness.

Var. *angustifolia* (Reich.) Not common. Shore, Deersound ; Oyce, Firth, &c. This variety, Mr Bennett says, is the same as var. *stenophylla* of Asch. and Græbn.

409. Z. nana (Roth.), *Dwarf Grass-wrack.*

This plant is given in H. C. Watson's list, on the authority of Syme. It is a plant likely to grow in Orkney, but has not been found recently, so far as I know.

Order LIII.—ORCHIDACEÆ.

Genus CXCIV.—ORCHIS (Linn.)

410. O. mascula (Linn.), *Early Purple Orchis.*

Westness, Rousay ; Hoy. The only place where I have gathered it was on the sea-banks, Berstane. Glen of Gair, Hoy ; south-west of Kame of Hoy (1883).

411. O. MACULATA (Linn.), *Spotted Hand-orchis.* Common.

Var. *O. ericetorum* (Linton). I found this in White Moss, St. Andrews. Mr Ar. Bennett says it seems a narrow-leaved *f.* of Linton's plant. See "Journal of Botany," 1901, p. 272, where a description of this plant is given by Linton. Linton's plant was evidently found in Orkney, as Mr Bennett gives it as an addition to Orkney flora. (See additions in "Ann. of Scot. Nat. Hist.," July 1908.)

412. O. LATIFOLIA (Linn.), *Marsh-orchis.*

Not so common as the last. My specimens are from Westray.

413. O. INCARNATA (Linn.), *Marsh-orchis.* Scarce.

Deerness; Hoy, in marsh at Orgill in 1900, plentiful, and no doubt elsewhere (Rev. E. S. Marshall).

Var. *O. angustifolia.* I found this variety in Deerness, near Bay of Newark (20th June 1909).

GENUS CXCV.—HABENARIA (Willd.)

414. H. CONOPSEA (Benth.), *Fragrant Orchis.* Fairly common.

Scapa; Caldale, St. Ola; Deerness, &c.

415. H. ALBIDA (Rich.), *White Orchis.*

Scarce, but pretty well distributed over Mainland —Scapa; Finstown; Maeshowe; Horraquoy, Deerness; Tankerness, &c.

416. H. VIRIDIS (Br.), *Frog-orchis.*   Scarce.

Houton (Syme); Standing Stones (Dr Fortescue); fairly common between Gloup and Brough, Deerness. I have specimens gathered in Westray (1905).

Genus CXCVI.—LISTERA (Br.)

417. L. CORDATA (Br.), *Tway-blade.*   Rare.

Hoy, Evie, Rousay, Orphir.   My specimens are from near Kame, Hoy; and from Orphir, sent by J. Omond, teacher.

418. L. OVATA (Br.), *Tway-blade.*   Scarce.

Wideford Burn (1900, M. Spence); Seatter, St. Ola ; Quendale, Rousay (G. Robson). I find this species is more numerous than the previous one.

Genus CXCVII.—GOODYERA (Br.)

419. G. REPENS (Br.), *Creeping Goodyera.*   Very rare.

Dr Grant sent me one plant which he found near Stairwaddy, Stromness. Mr Ar. Bennett says:—" The finding of a single specimen cannot be considered as admitting the plant as an Orcadian species. Still there is no reason why it should not grow as far north, as it occurs throughout Sweden up to Lapland ; in North and South Norway ; and is distributed throughout Finland and Lapland, except the four northern provinces, in which few stations are on record. It occurs in West Ross, East and West Sutherland, but is not on record for Caithness or the Outer Hebrides. Prof. Trail says:—" In Scotland, so far as I have seen, it is almost absolutely restricted to woods of conifers; hence its occurrence in Orkney is unexpected." Since the above appeared in the "Ann. of Scot. Nat. Hist.," Dr Fortescue told me that he remembers some one bringing a plant to Dr Boswell, who resided then at Swanbister. He said it was *Goodyera repens.* Mrs Wm. Evans, Edinburgh, found one in Harray in July 1874, as reported in "Ann. of Scot. Nat. Hist.," No. 70, p. 123. Dr Nordstedt, of Lund, writes:—" I have seen *Goodyera* abundant on the west coast of Norway, in open ground, where the air is very moist, and I think *Goodyera* can grow in open ground in Orkney, as the air is probably damp enough there."

ORDER LIV.—IRIDACEÆ.

GENUS CXCVIII.—IRIS (Linn.)

420. I. PSEUDACORUS (Linn.), *Iris.* Common.

ORDER LV.—LILIACEÆ.

GENUS CXCIX.—SCILLA (Linn.), *Squill.*

421. S. VERNA (Huds.) Common.

Some pretty flowers of *Scilla* have been found— white, purple, pink, &c. The prettiest have been got in Eday.

GENUS CC.—NARTHECIUM (Huds.) *Bog-asphodel.*

422. N. OSSIFRAGUM (Huds.) Common.
Orkney name, "Pulderucks."

ORDER LVI.—JUNCACEÆ.

GENUS CCI.—JUNCUS (Linn.)

423. J. TRIGLUMIS (Linn.), *Three-flowered Rush.* Scarce.

Ward Hill, Orphir; above Naversdale. My specimen was gathered by G. W. Scarth, in Birsay (Sept. 1909).

424. J. BIGLUMIS (Linn.), *Two-flowered Rush.* Scarce.

Above Naversdale. I have never seen this plant; no authority.

425. J. BUFONIUS (Linn.), *Toad Rush.* Common.

426. J. EFFUSUS (Linn.), *Common Rush.* Common.

Var. *spiralis.* This variety is pretty common in Orkney. I sent a short communication regarding it to the Edinburgh Botanical Society, per Prof. J. Bayley Balfour in 1906. In a note appended to my communication it is stated that this is probably the first record of its occurrence in a wild form in Scotland.

427. J. CONGLOMERATUS (Linn.), *Common Rush.* Common.

428. J. SQUARROSUS (Linn.), *Heath Rush.* Common.

429. J. GERARDI (Loisel). Not uncommon.

It is generally found in salt marshes, as at the school, St. Andrews.

430. J. BULBOSUS (Linn,) Common.

Var. *fluitans* was got in Loch Sabiston, Birsay; seen by Mr Ar. Bennett. Var. *uliginosum* (Sibth.) was got in St. Andrews, near White Moss; also seen by Mr Ar. Bennett.

431. J. LAMPOCARPUS (Ehrh.), *Shining Rush*, Common.

432. J, NITRITELLUS (Don.), *Shining Rush*.
Kirbuster Loch, Orphir (Dr Fortescue's list).

433. J. ACUTIFLORUS (Ehrh.), *Jointed Rush*. Not uncommon.

434. J. COMPRESSUS (Jacq.)

This plant is given in "Florula Orcadensis" on the authority of Syme and Neill, and published in H. C. Watson's list, but not in Dr Fortescue's. I have not found it.

GENUS CCII.—LUZULA.

435. L, PILOSA (Willd.), *Wood-rush*.

Dry pastures (Dr Duguid and R. Heddle). This plant has not been reported for many years, and one is apt to conclude that a mistake has been made. The plant is likely to grow in Orkney. Mr Patrick Neill records it from Rousay under the title of *Juncus pilosus*. I have specimens from Dr Flett from near Edinburgh. It is so unlike any other plant that it is hardly possible a mistake could have been made.

436. L. SYLVATICA (Gaud.), *Wood-rush*. Common.
It is found by sides of streams in hilly districts.

437. L. CAMPESTRIS (DC.), *Field Wood-rush.*
Common.

438. L. MULTIFLORA (DC.), *Field Wood-rush.*
Common.

Var. *conjesta* (Lej.) Common (Dr Boswell).
Var. *sudetica* (DC.) Common on heaths (Dr Boswell).

ORDER LVII.—CYPERACEÆ.

GENUS CCIII.—SCHOENUS (Linn.), *Bog-rush.*

439. S. NIGRICANS (Linn.) Common in wet bogs.

Var. *nana* (Lange). This var. was named by Lange from specimens sent from Shetland by Mr Beeby. I found some in bog land belonging to Mr Seatter, Post Office, near Park, Deerness. Mr G. Scarth tells me he found the shore of Starray Loch, Birsay, covered with it in some places.

GENUS CCIV.—ELEOCHARIS (Br.)

440. E. PALUSTRIS (Roem and Schult), *Spike-rush.*
Common.

441. E. UNIGLUMIS (Link.), *Creeping Spike-rush.*
Rare.

The Fidge, Swanbister (Dr Boswell). The plant I have from where bog, Myrkaday, enters the sea is, I think, this. It is given in Watson's "Florula Orcadensis" on the authority of Syme. I sent a plant to Mr Ar. Bennett, which I took to be this. He wrote :—" The *Scirpus* does look like *uniglumis*, but it is hardly in good fruit condition to be sure."

442. E. MULTICAULIS (Sm.), *Spike-rush.*
Marshes above Ryssa, Walls (Dr Boswell).

GENUS CCV.—SCIRPUS (Linn.), *Club-rush.*
443. S. LACUSTRIS (Linn.), *Bul-rush.*
In lochs of Aikerness; Newark, Sanday; Bosquoy, Harray; Banks, Birsay; Wasbister, Rousay.

444. S. TABERNÆMONTANI (Gmel.), *Bul-rush.* Rare.
Burn of Scapa (Dr Duguid), Loch of Græmeshall (29th July 1910, M. Spence).

445. S. SETACEUS (Linn.), *Bristle Mud-rush.* Not frequent.
My specimens are from Berriedale, Hoy, per Dr Flett; from bog above Wood Cottage, Deerness; and from bog below Ocilster, Holm.

446. S. FLUITANS (Linn.), *Floating Mud-rush.* Not common.
Walls; Loch of Knitchin, Rousay. Dr Grant sent me specimens from near Stromness.

447. S. PAUCIFLORIS (Lightf.), *Spike-rush.*
Harray (Prof. Trail). Fairly abundant on hill between Syradale and Redland, Firth.

448. S. CÆSPITOSUS (Linn.), *Scaly Spike-rush.* Common.

GENUS CCVI.—ERIOPHORUM (Linn.), *Cotton-grass.*
449. E. VAGINATUM (Linn.), *Cotton-grass.* Common.

450. E. ANGUSTIFOLIUM (Roth.), *Common Cotton-grass.* Common.

G

GENUS CCVII.—BLYSMUS (Panz.), *Blysmus.*

451. B. RUFUS (Link.) Rare.

Near Rackwick; Wauk Mill Bay; behind Piero-wall; and in salt marsh near school, St. Andrews. I have specimens from all except Rackwick.

ORDER LVIII.—CAREX, *Sedge.*

452. C. DIOICA (Linn.) Not uncommon.

Braebuster, Deerness; Scapa (Dr Boswell); Hoy (R. Heddle).

453. C. PULICARIS (Linn.), *Flea Sedge.* Common.

454. C. PAUCIFLORA (Lightf.), *Few-flowered Sedge.* Rare.

Rousay (R. Heddle). I have never found it, although I have looked for it in many likely places on the Mainland.

455. C. INCURVA (Lightf.), *Curved Sedge.* Rare.

Pierowall; Newark, Deerness; Boardhouse, Birsay; Sandside, Deerness.

456. C. ARENARIA (Linn.), *Sand Sedge.*

This is one of our best sand-binders, and is common in suitable places.

457. C. PANICULATA (Linn.), *Great Sedge.*

Dr Fortescue reported this from Swanbister. I have found it near Quoykea, St. Andrews, but not growing well; but in a bog below school, Cross, Sanday, through which a ditch ran, it grew luxuriantly. It grows in bog below Caldale, St. Ola.

458. C. STELLULATA (Good), *Little Sedge*. Common.

459. C. MURICATA (Linn.), *Prickly Sedge*. Rare.

I found this once in passing from Bigswell Hill towards Heddle, in the valley near peat banks in the meadow below Germiston.

460. C. LEPORINA (Linn.), *Oval-spiked Sedge*. Fairly common.

It is often met with in pastures which have at one time been under cultivation.

461. C. RIGIDA (Good.), *Rigid Sedge*. Rare.
Hoy Hills. Dr Fortescue says he once found this. Dr Flett and I got it there, too. I found one plant on top of Kirbuster Hill, Birsay, in 1904.

462. C. VULGARIS (Fr.), *Common Sedge*. Common.

463. C. GLAUCA (Scop.), *Glaucous Heath Sedge*. Common.

464. C. PILULIFERA (Linn.), *Round-headed Sedge*. Fairly common.
Several places in Orphir (Dr Fortescue); Harray and Birsay (Prof. Trail). Dr Fortescue writes:—" I once found one fruiting stem of a *carex* in Ramsdale, Orphir, which I sent to Dr Boswell. He wrote :— ' Probably *pilulifera*, if not unknown to me.' It had a long bract, perhaps three inches in length."

465. C. VERNA (Chaix), *Vernal Sedge*.
Dry pastures (R. Heddle). I have never found it.

466. C. PANICEA (Linn.), *Pink-leaved Sedge.* Common.

467. C. BINERVIS (Sm.), *Green-ribbed Sedge.* Common.

468. C. LIMOSA (Linn.), *Mud Sedge.* Very rare.

G. W. Scarth found one patch on the hill between Hillside, Birsay, and Evie. I am not sure of the exact locality. This was in the summer of 1910.

469. C. DISTANS (Linn.), *Loose Sedge.*

Fidge, Swanbister (1849); extinct (?) (1875, Dr Boswell).

470. C. FULVA (Good.), *Tawny Sedge.* Common.

In Hooker this is given as a sub-species of *C. distans.* Dr Boswell gives var. *sterilis* as a var. of *fulva.* These are the only stations in Great Britain for this variety—marsh, Piggar, Swanbister, Orphir; near South Dam, Hoy. I have never seen it.

471. C. EXTENSA (Good.), *Long-bracteate Sedge.*

Fidge, Swanbister (1849, Dr Boswell). It is growing extensively in salt marsh near school, St. Andrews; and in Kettletoft Bay, Sanday.

472. C. FLAVA (Linn.), *Yellow Sedge.* Common.

Var. *lepidocarpa* (Tausch), (Dr Boswell). *Lepidocarpa* × *Hornschuchiana* is given as a hybrid found in Orkney by Rev. E. S. Marshall in "Ann. Scot. Nat. Hist.," Jan. 1910, p. 48.

473. C. Œderi (Retz), *Yellow Sedge.* Fairly common.

474. C. ROSTRATA (Stokes), *Bladder Sedge.* Common. This plant is better known as *C. ampullacea.*

ORDER LIX.—GRAMINEÆ.

GENUS CCVIII.—ANTHOXANTHUM (Linn.), *Vernal-grass.*

475. A. ODORATUM (Linn.) Common.

GENUS CCIX.—PHALARIS (Linn.), *Reed-grass.*

476. P. ARUNDINACEA (Linn.) Local; fairly common.

GENUS CCX.—ALOPECURUS (Linn.), *Fox-tail-grass.*

477. A. GENICULATUS (Linn.) Common.

478. A. PRATENSIS (Linn.), *Common Fox-tail-grass.* Not uncommon. My specimens are from Holm, below U.F. Church; and Braebuster.

GENUS CCXI.—PHLEUM (Linn.), *Cat's-tail-grass.*

479. P. PRATENSE (Linn.) Not uncommon.

Edge of cornfield, Bu, Hoy (Col. H. H. Johnston, C.B.)

GENUS CCXII.—AGROSTIS (Linn.), *Bent-grass.*

480. A. CANINA (Linn.)

Hoy Hills (1880, Dr Boswell); near Gloup, Deerness (1910, M. Spence); Holm Hills (1910, M. Spence). Mr Bennett says:—" I have never seen so dark a form of *canina* as those you sent, neither can I find any variety so named."

481. A. ALBA (Linn.), *Marsh Bent-grass.* Common.

G. W. Scarth tells me he got a variety which Mr Bennett considers a small state of *coarctata* (Hoffm.)

Var. *stolonifera.* Sands in various places (R. Heddle). In a rill near trees, Carrick, Eday (M. Spence, Sept. 1908).

482. A. VULGARIS (With.), *Fine Bent-grass.* Common.

Var. *pumila* (Lightf.) Fairly common; Deerness, Firth, &c.

GENUS CCXIII.—AMMOPHILA (Host.), *Sea-reed.*

483. A. ARUNDINACEA (Host.) Common.

Sandy shores; Deerness, Sanday, Walls, &c.

GENUS CCXIV.—PHRAGMITES, *Common Reed.*

484. P. COMMUNIS (Trin.) Fairly common.

Braebuster, Deerness; Loch of Harray (Dr Boswell); Loch Isbister, Birsay.

GENUS CCXV.—DESCHAMPSIA (Beauv.), *Hair-grass.*

485. D. CÆSPITOSA (Linn.), *Tufted Hair-grass.* Common.

486. D. FLEXUOSA (Linn.), *Wavy Hair-grass.* Common on heaths.

GENUS CCXVI.—AIRA (Linn.)

487. A. CARYOPHYLLEA (Linn.), *Silver Hair-grass.* Common.

Generally found on poor cultivated soil.

488. A. PRÆCOX (Linn.), *Early Hair-grass.* Common.

GENUS CCXVII.—AVENA (Linn)., *Oat-grass.*

489. A. PUBESCENS (Huds.), *Downy Oat-grass.* Scarce.

Manse of Hoy and Scapa (Dr Boswell); Gills of Scapa (Dr Gillies).

490. A. PRATENSIS (Linn.), *Narrow-leaved Oat-grass.* Doubtful (D. Macnab).

491. A. STRIGOSA (Schreb.), *Bristle Oat-grass.* Introduced.

492. A. FATUA (Linn.), *Wild Oat-grass.* Introduced.

GENUS CCXVIII.—ARRHENATHERUM (Beauv.)

493. A. AVENACEUM (Beauv.), *False Oat-grass.* Common.

Var. *bulbosum* (Presl.) Common.

The variety is a weed which in impoverished lands becomes a very disagreeable pest. In Orkney it is named "swine-beads," probably because pigs rutted them up and fed on them.

GENUS CCXIX.—TRISETUM (Pers.), *Yellow Oat-grass.*

494. T. PRATENSE (Pers.) Not common.
Fields; sandy spots (R. Heddle).

GENUS CCXX.—HOLCUS (Linn.), *Soft-grass.*

495. H. MOLLIS (Linn.)

Dr Duguid and R. Heddle say it is common; but this is probably a mistake.

496. H. LANATUS (Linn.), *Yorkshire Fog.* Very common.

Called "punds" in Orkney. Tethers and bridle reins were often wrought of long meadow grasses, as *Holcus lanatus,* says Mr Pat. Neill.

GENUS CCXXI.—SIEGLINGIA (Bernh.), *Heath-grass.*

497. S. DECUMBENS (Bernh.) Fairly common on dry pastures.

GENUS CCXXII.—MOLINIA (Schrank.)

498. M. CŒRULEA (Moench), *Purple Molinia.* Local; not uncommon.

GENUS CCXXIII.—CATABROSA.

499. C. AQUATICA (Beauv.), *Water Whorl-grass.* Local, but fairly common.

Loch of Aikerness; Barns, Deerness, &c. Var. *minor* is, I think, the more common.

GENUS CCXXIV.—GLYCERIA (Br.)

500. G. FLUITANS (Br.), *Floating Meadow-grass.* Common.

501. G. PLICATA (Fries.), *Floating Meadow-grass.*

Near Learquoy, Orphir (1849, Dr Boswell); bog, Mirkaday, Deerness.

GENUS CCXXV.—SCLEROCHLOA (Beauv.)

502. S. MARITIMA (Lindl.), *Sea Meadow-grass.* Local.

Firth; Sebay Mill; and in suitable localities by the sea.

503. S. DISTANS (Bab.), *Reflexed Meadow-grass.*
Ayre at Kirkwall (Dr Duguid).

GENUS CCXXVI.—POA (Linn.), *Annual Meadow-grass.*

504. P. ANNUA (Linn.) Common.

505. P. COMPRESSA (Linn.), *Flat-stalked Meadow-grass.*
Sides of roads (Dr Duguid and R. Heddle's list).

506. P. PRATENSIS (Linn.), *Smooth Meadow-grass.*
Fairly common.

507. P. TRIVIALIS (Linn.), *Rough Meadow-grass.*
Fairly common.

GENUS CCXXVII.— BRIZA (Linn.), *Quaking-grass.*

508. B. MEDIA (Linn.)
Hill pastures above Westness (R. Heddle); Wideford; Swanbister; Binscarth, &c.

GENUS CCXXVIII.—CYNOSURUS (Linn.), *Dog's-tail-grass.*

509. C. CRISTATUS (Linn.) Common.

GENUS CCXXIX.—DACTYLIS (Linn.), *Cock's-foot-grass.*

510. D. GLOMERATA (Linn.)
Introduced, and now frequently met with along fields, ditches, and dykes.

GENUS CCXXX.—FESTUCA (Linn.), *Fescue-grass.*

511. F. BROMOIDES (Linn.)
Sides of farm buildings (Dr Duguid and Dr Boswell). My specimen is from Rousay.

512. F. OVINA (Linn.), *Sheep's Fescue-grass.* Common.

Var. *vivipara.* Fairly common on wet moors.

513. F. RUBRA (Linn.), *Creeping Fescue-grass.* Not uncommon.

At anemometer, Deerness, &c.

514. F. ELATIOR (Sm.), *Tall Fescue-grass.*

Holms of Wasbister, Harray Loch; meadows near Kirkwall.

515. F. PRATENSIS (Huds.), *Meadow Fescue-grass.* Not common.

Pastures; Smiddybanks, Deerness, &c.

Var. *loliacea* (Curt.), *Spiked Fescue.* Meadows (Dr Neill).

GENUS CCXXXI.—BROMUS.

516. B. STERILIS (Linn.), *Barren Brome-grass.* Not uncommon (R. Heddle).

Doubtless a mistake (Dr Fortescue). I have not found it.

517. B. SECALINUS (Bab.), *Rye Brome-grass.*
Corn fields (R. Heddle).
Var. *velutinus* (Schrad.) Common (R. Heddle).

518. B. RACEMOSUS (Parl.), *Smooth Brome-grass.* Common.

519. B. HORDEACEUS (Linn.), *Soft Brome-grass.* Common.

Var. *glabrescens* (Gren.) Not common. Mr Bennett considers that this var. is intermediate between *glabrescens* and *hordeaceus* (Fries.) He saw specimens.

GENUS CCXXXII.—BRACHYPODIUM (Beauv.)

520. B. SYLVATICUM (Beauv.), *False Brome-grass.*

Scapa (Dr Boswell) ; Berstane (Dr Duguid) ; Hobister (R. Heddle).

GENUS CCXXXIII.—TRITICUM (Linn.)

521. T. CANINUM (Linn.), *Wheat-grass.*

Corn fields, Upper Hobister (R. Heddle) ; Howan (Prof. Trail) ; Deerness (M. Spence).

522. T. REPENS (Linn.), *Couch-grass.* Common.

Var. *barbata.* Common.

523. T. ACUTUM (DC.), *Wheat-grass.*

Recorded by Dr Boswell—Scapa ; Hoxa Links.

524. T. JUNCEUM (Linn.), *Rusky Wheat-grass.* Rather searce.

Scapa ; Swanbister ; Hoxa ; Bay of Newark, Deerness.

GENUS CCXXXIV.—LOLIUM (Linn.)

525. L. PERENNE (Linn.), *Rye-grass.* Common— introduced.

GENUS CCXXXV.—ELYMUS (Linn.), *Lime-grass.*

526. E. ARENARIUS.

Hoy ; Hoxa ; rather scarce (Dr Boswell). Sandside, Deerness ; Breckness ; Biggings, Stenness ; Walls ; Holm, &c., local.

GENUS CCXXXVI.—NARDUS.

527. N. STRICTA (Linn.), *Mat-grass.* Common.

Class III.—CRYPTOGAMEÆ.

Order LX.—FILICES.

Genus CCXXXVII.—POLYPODIUM (Linn.), *Polypody.*

528. P. VULGARE (Linn.)   Fairly common.

Berriedale ; Rousay ; Orphir ; Gillsburn, Scapa ; Stromness ; Brough, Deerness, &c.

Genus CCXXXVIII.—HYMENOPHYLLUM (Sm.)

529. H. WILSONI (Hook.), *Filmy Fern.*   Rare.

Hoy Hill and meadow of the Kame—the only known stations. It is so like a moss that it may readily be mistaken for one.

Genus CCXXXIX.—PTERIS (Linn.), *Bracken.*

530. P. AQUILINA (Linn.)   Common.

Genus CCXL.—BLECHNUM (Linn.), *Hard Fern.*

531. B. SPICANT (With.)   Common.

Genus CCXLI. —ASPLENIUM (Linn.), *Spleenwort.*

532. A. ADIANTUM-NIGRUM (Linn.)   Rare and local.

Rousay ; Evie ; Westray ; Syradale ; Hoy ; Harray. Gathered by me in Rousay in 1894.

533. A. Trichomanes (Linn.), *Common Spleenwort.* Local ; rather rare.

Hoy ; Evie ; Rousay ; Westray ; Harray. Gathered by me in Rousay in 1894.

534. A. Ruta-muraria (Linn.), *Wall Rue.* Rare. Ward Hill, Rousay.

535. A. marinum (Linn.), *Sea Spleenwort.* Fairly common.

Scapa ; Hobister ; Deerness ; Head of Holland. This fern is generally found where there is a sea cliff exposure of red or yellow sandstone.

Genus CCXLII.—ATHYRIUM (Roth.)

536. A. Filix-fœmina (Roth.), *Lady Fern.* Common.

Var. *A. rhæticum* (Roth.) J. Spence, Overabist, Hillside, Birsay, reports this variety from his neighbourhood.

Genus CCXLIII.—PHYLLITIS (Hill), *Hart's-tongue.*

537. P. Scolopendrium (Greene).

I am afraid this fern is now extinct, or very nearly so, in Orkney. It at one time grew in Rousay, Eynhallow, and Hoy. Mrs Anderson, Manse, Hoy, found the last known one on the cliffs to the east of Dwarfie Stone.

Genus CCXLIV.—CYSTOPTERIS (Bernh.), *Bladder Fern.*

538. C. fragilis (Bernh.) Local and scarce.

Hoy ; Rousay ; Fitty Hill, Westray ; Redland, Firth ; and in shaded places on other hills.

Genus CCXLV.—POLYSTICHUM (Roth.)

539. P. LONCHITIS (Roth.), *Holly Fern.*

I have two fronds of this. The first was got per Dr Grant from Mrs Anderson, Manse, Hoy, who found the fern in one of the gullies on north side of Ward Hill about 1900. The other was got from G. W. Scarth, who found it in fair abundance on east shoulder of Ward Hill. This was in 1908.

540. P. ACULEATUM (Roth.), *Prickly Shield Fern.* Rare and local.

Hoy (Dr Boswell).

Var. *lobatum* (Presl.) Wooded burn, west of old church, Hoy (Dr Grant).

Genus CCXLVI.—LASTREA (Presl.)

541. L. FILIX-MAS (Presl.), *Male Fern.* Common.

Var. *Borreri* (Newm.), *Male Fern.* Rather scarce. My specimen was got on north side of Ward Hill, Hoy.

542. L. SPINULOSA (Presl.)

Var. *exaltata* (Syme). Waulk Mill Bay (October 1906). Seen by Mr Ar. Bennett.

Var. *decipiens* (Syme). Seen by Mr Ar. Bennett, who said it was this. Got at Redland (1905).

543. L. DILATATA (Presl.), *Buckler Fern.* Common. Var. *alpina.* Orphir; Stenness (Dr Boswell).

544. L. ÆMULA (Brack.), *Buckler Fern.*

Not uncommon in Orphir and South Isles. Mr Ar. Bennett says :—" I have several fine specimens gathered by Dr Boswell on west side of Waulk Mill Bay in 1875." I got several near Waulk Mill in 1903, and burn, Redland, Firth, in 1905.

545. L. OREOPTERIS (Presl.), *Mountain Fern*. Rare. Orphir and Hoy (Dr Boswell).

GENUS CCXLVII.—BOTRYCHIUM (Sw.), *Moonwort*.

546. B. LUNARIA (Sw.)

Var. *incisum* (Milde). Fairly well scattered over the Mainland and islands—Stenness; Deerness; Orphir. Var. *incisum* is, I think, the more common form in Orkney.

GENUS CCXLVIII.—OPHIOGLOSSUM (Linn.),
Adder's-tongue.

547. O. VULGATUM (Linn.)

Var. *ambiguum*. Scarce. Orphir ; Flotta ; Calf of Ryssa ; Hunda ; Hoy ; Eday ; Dounby ; Calf of Cava. Dr Fortescue says :—" Among short grass on the top of the sea-banks only where the grass is cropped short by sheep. On one spot the grass was allowed to grow rank, and the adder's-tongue disappeared."

ORDER LXI.—LYCOPODIACEÆ.

GENUS CCXLIX.—LYCOPODIUM (Linn.), *Club-moss*.

548. L. CLAVATUM (Linn.) Fairly common.
Hoy ; Mainland ; Rousay.

549. L. ANNOTINUM (Linn.), *Club-moss*. Local ; scarcer than the last.

Berriedale, Hoy. Gathered in 1904 by myself ;

reported by Col. H. H. Johnston, C.B., and Dr Fortescue.

550. L. ALPINUM (Linn.), *Alpine Club-moss*. Rare.

I have seen it above U.F. Manse, Evie; Bigswell Hill, Stenness; Wideford Hill, and Harray.

551. L. INUNDATUM (Linn.), *Marsh Club-moss*.

Near Pegal Burn, Walls (1848, R. Heddle). I have not got a specimen of this.

552. L. SELAGO (Linn.), *Fir Club-moss*. Common.

ORDER LXII.—SELAGINELLACEÆ.

GENUS CCL.—SELAGINELLA (Spring).

553. S. SELAGINOIDES (Gray). Common.

GENUS CCLI.—ISOETES (Linn.)

554. I. LACUSTRIS (Linn.), *Quill-wort*.

Said to be found in loch on Knitchin Hill, Rousay; Carness; Orphir. There is some doubt attached to this. Dr Fortescue says :—"I have often looked for it in Orkney, but never found it. I have seen it on shores of lochs on the Grampians." Dr Boswell remarks, "Likely only *Littorella*."

ORDER LXIII.—EQUISETACEÆ, *Horse-tail*.

GENUS CCLII.—EQUISETUM (Linn.)

555. E. ARVENSE (Linn.), *Corn Horse-tail*. Common.

556. E. SYLVATICUM (Linn.), *Wood Horse-tail.* Local; rather scarce.

557. E. PALUSTRE (Linn.), *Marsh Horse-tail.* Common.

558. E. LIMOSUM (Linn.), *Smooth Naked Horse-tail.* Common.

559. E. PRATENSE (Ehrh.), *Blunt Horse-tail.*

This horse-tail is pretty common in Deerness and Upper Sanday, St. Andrews. It was unknown in Orkney till a few years ago. Mr Ar. Bennett says:— "This is a very interesting addition to Orkney flora. It does not occur in Shetland nor the Færoes, but is found in Iceland and Sweden."

ORDER LXIV.—CHARACEÆ.

GENUS CCLIII.—NITELLA (Agardh).

560. N. OPACA (Agardh). Fairly common. Swanbister, Rennibister, near Stromness, &c.

GENUS CCLIV.—CHARA (Linn.)

561. C. FRAGILIS (Desv.) Fairly common.

Var. *delicatula.* Plentiful round shores of Loch Harray (Dr Fortescue).

Var. approaching *barbata.* Shallow pools north-west of Stones of Stenness (Dr Fortescue's list).

562. C. ASPERA (Willd.)

Skail, Harray Loch, Papa Westray, Holm.

H

Var. *subinermis* (Kuetz.) Abundant in deeper water of Loch of Harray. Dr Clouston says of this species in "Anderson's Guide" :—" This is the only addition to the Orkney flora which is new to Great Britain."

563. C. HISPIDA (Linn.)

Loch of Airy, Stronsay ; Brodgar.

564. C. VULGARIS (Linn.) Common.

Var. *longibracteata* (Kuetz.) Kirbuster, Orphir ; Holm ; seen by Mr Ar. Bennett.

Var. *atrovirens* (Lowe). Swanbister.

565. C. BALTICA (Fr.)

This *chara* was found for the first time some twelve years ago by the late Mr W. Crawford, Edinburgh. It grows luxuriantly and abundantly in the muddy bottom of the Loch of Stenness.

PLANTS USED MEDICINALLY

AND THEIR APPLICATION BY
ORCADIANS.

BUCK-BEAN or BOG-BEAN, *Menyanthes trifoliata.*

Locally known as "craw-shoe." The leaves were used instead of hops to give bitterness to the wort of home-brewed ale ; and the bruised leaves were applied to the sores of scrofula. It was also used to flavour ale in Birsay. In Deerness it was given to cattle suffering from tuberculosis.

COLTSFOOT, *Tussilago Farfara.*

The leaves were partly dried, put in a clean clay pipe and smoked in the same way as tobacco, to cure bronchitis, coughs, &c., the smoke being inhaled. A sweetened decoction of the flowers was also used for colds.

CHAMOMILE, *Anthemis nobilis.*

An infusion of this was used for bilious troubles; and the flowers steeped in hot water were applied as poultices for soothing pain in inflammation. These were called " camavine flooers."

LESSER CELANDINE, *Ranunculus Ficaria.*

A decoction of the leaves was used for bathing purposes in cases of piles.

CHICKWEED, *Stellaria media.*

The leaves when bruised were applied as poultices in cases of inflammation.

WATER-CRESS, *Nasturtium officinale.*

This was one of the very few plants eaten in an uncooked state by Orcadians.

DANDELION, *Taraxacum officinale.*

A decoction of the roots was taken for stomach and liver affections; the flowers also were infused, and the sweetened infusion taken for colds.

DOCK, *Rumex.*

The juice of the stem expressed proved a thorough antidote to the sting of the nettle. Selected stems of *Rumex aquaticus* were woven into an engine called a "fursaclew" for catching trout.

ELDER, *Sambucus nigra.*

The berries were boiled with sugar in a quantity of water. To this, when cold, a small quantity of brandy or whisky was added. It was then bottled and kept for after consumption as elder-berry wine.

ELECAMPANE, *Inula helenium.*

A decoction of the root sweetened with sugar was given to children suffering from whooping-cough.

EYE-BRIGHT, *Euphrasia officinalis.*

The juice of this plant was dropped into the eye to check inflammation.

PURGING FLAX, *Linum catharticum.*

A decoction of this was administered as an aperient.

FOXGLOVE, *Digitalis purpurea.*

Strict injunctions were laid upon the goose-herd not to allow the goslings to eat of the leaves, for if they did partake, death soon followed, thus showing the poisonous nature of the plant.

FUMITORY, *Fumaria officinalis.*

The juice of this was given to children as a cure for worms; also to foals for the same purpose, but in much larger doses, of course.

GENTIAN, *Gentiana campestris.*

A decoction of this was given in considerable quantities as a supposed cure for gravel. It was also considered a valuable tonic, while an infusion of the dried plant was credited with the highest curative properties in all attacks of jaundice, except the " black" kind, which was looked upon as incurable.

THRIFT, *Statice Armeria.*

Its thick, tuberous roots, sliced and boiled with milk, were highly prized in Orkney as a remedy in pulmonary consumption.

GERMANDER SAGE, *Teucrium Scorodonia.*

The leaves were dried and took the place of hops in the ale brewings. Jaundice was supposed to be cured by an infusion of the leaves.

GROUND IVY, *Nepeta Glechoma.*

This being dried, was infused, and the infusion was taken like tea as a stimulant.

GOUT WEED, *Ægopodium Podagraria.*

Roots and leaves having been boiled, the affected part, in cases of gout, sciatica, or hip-joint disease, was fomented with the decoction.

MUGWORT, *Artemisia vulgaris.*

The leaves when dried were smoked in a pipe as a substitute for tobacco. It was so used in most parishes.

"*Artemisia vulgaris,*" P. Neill says, "is called 'grey bulwand' in Orkney. The tops of the stalks of the plant are used by the common people in place of hops."

THE NETTLE, *Utrica dioica.*

The tender leaves were boiled, and, sauced with butter, were eaten with bere bread. They were also put as a vegetable in broth before the cabbage was ready. *Utrica dioica* and *urens* were used for rheumatism. A decoction was made from it, and drunk by the sufferer. It is said to have been often efficacious. Nettle ale was also made ; and I believe there are some people still living who have partaken of it.

PLANTAIN, *Plantago major.*

In severe abrasions of the skin, the broad leaf was applied under the bandage to allay the immediate pain, and to prevent suppuration or blood-poisoning.

SNEEZE-WORT, *Achillea ptarmica.*

An infusion of the flowers and leaves was in common use as a refreshment after meals. In Birsay the flowers of this plant were used for tea.

SORREL, *Rumex acetosa* and *acetosella,*

The leaves were chewed because of their pleasant acidity, and for mitigating thirst.

CORN-SPURREY, *Spergula arvensis,* and *sativa.*

The little brown seeds, locally known as " reuth," were ground and made into porridge during a scarcity of meal.

SUN-SPURGE, *Euphorbia helioscopia.*

The white, milky-like fluid in the hollow stem was applied to warts to remove them, hence the local name, " warty-girse."

TANSY, *Tanacetum vulgare.*

A decoction of this was administered in doses to children troubled with worms.

TORMENTIL, *Potentilla tormentilla.*

Locally termed " hill-barks." The roots were scraped, and boiled in milk, and the liquid used as a cure for diarrhœa. A strong decoction of the roots was also used as a substitute for bark in the tanning of skins—hence the local name, probably.

WORMWOOD, *Artemisia absinthium.*

An infusion of the leaves was given for dyspepsia and for worms. It was grown in most gardens or yards. The whole leaves, stems, and flowers were boiled, and the juice bottled and drunk when cooled. It was used as a tonic. It was also used as a preservative from moths. Stalks were placed in the blanket-chest.

YARROW, or MILLFOIL. *Achillea millefolium.*

The dried flowers were infused, and the liquid drunk as a stimulant like tea. Mr Pat. Neill says: —"At Kerbuster, Deerness, I observed laid out to dry a large collection of flowering tops of the dwarfy millfoil (*Achillea millefolia*)."

SMEROWS, *Trifoliam repens.*

To find a four-partite clover-leaf was considered a good omen. It was used as one of the most common of Orcadian charms. It brought luck on all occasions and in all circumstances. Mr Delday, poet, Deerness, pointed out one of the most efficacious of its charms when he said that his mother bade him, on the occasion of the Lammas Market, Kirkwall, look for a *smerow* and put it in his boot till the market was over, for then the "cheap Johns" would not be able to cheat him, whilst he at the same time would be enabled to see through all their sleights of art; and, in addition, no wily spinster would be able to captivate him.

YELLOW IRIS, *Iris Pseud-acorus.*

The raw juice from the roots of this plant was used to cure toothache. The juice was sucked up the nose.

Juncus Effusus.

The pith was extracted from these and used in the old oil lamp (*cruisie*) as a wick. This and *conglomeratus* were also cut and neatly tied up in "baets" for winding in the winter evenings for "bands" and "fettles" for "caeseys," and other purposes.

Dr Wallace in 1700 says :—

"The more common and general diseases are the Scurvy, Agues, Consumptions, &c. Commonly in the spring they (Orcadians) are troubled with an Aguish Distemper which they call the *Axes*, but for this there are *Quacks* amongst them that pretend an infallible Cure by way of Diet-Drink, infusing a hotch potch of several plants (I suppose what are greenest at the time) in an English gallon of ale ; the receipt is this. They take of Buckhorn plantain, Water plantain, Lovage, wild Daisie, Rocket, roots of Elecampane, Millefoil, roots of Spignell, Dandelyon, Parsley roots, Wormwood, Cumfrey, Tansey, Sea pink, Garden Angelica, and a kind of Masterwort, the *imperatorie affinis ;* of all these they take a like quantity, to wit, about half a handful, and of this infusion they drink half a pint morning and evening. This is what they call *Axes grass,* and the old women talk wonders of it, pretending there are so many of the herbs good for the liver, so many for the head, and so many for the heart, spleen, &c.

"In phthisical distempers they use Arby or thrift boiled with sweet milk."

Lovage — *Ligusticum Scoticum ;* Rocket—*Cakile maritima.* Masterwort, Spignell, and Comfrey were garden plants ; Arby was Seathrift.

LIST OF ORKNEY MOSSES
(V.C. 111.)

INTRODUCTION.

FOR the information of the general reader, I may explain that the British Isles, excluding Ireland, are for Bryological purposes divided into 112 Vice-Counties and 18 Provinces. The Outer Hebrides (V.C. 110), the Orkneys (V.C. 111), and the Shetlands (V.C. 112), form the North Isles Province (P. XVIII.), because from their physical characteristics being similar, their moss floras would be identical, and of the lowland type.

The mosses in this list were gathered by me in the West Mainland of Orkney and in the islands of Hoy, Græmsay, and Flotta (V.C. 111). Additional records and their sources are given in the supplement. The arrangement of the list follows that of the "Census Catalogue of British Mosses," published

in 1907.   Omissions in the sequences of the numbers
in the list bear reference to the numbers recorded in
the Catalogue which have not, within my knowledge,
been found in Orkney.   Probably some of these
blanks may be filled by careful exploration in
woods and in hilly situations.   I have stated the
localities of plants which I found were more or less
rare in my limited areas of investigation.   Drainage
is influencing the frequency of some of the water-
loving species.   *Climacium dendroides*—a fine, tree-
like plant—lately found growing in three localities
in Stromness, is now, from the cause stated, reduced
to its last bog, west of the mouth of Garson Burn.
Additions by immigration may also occur.   In the
month of January last I found *Barbula Hornschuchiana* and *Amblystegium Juratzkanum,* both probably
introduced, growing on the pier at Ness, Stromness.
The previous furthest north recorded station for the
first-named plant was East Perth (V.C. 96), and for
the last-named Easter-Ness and Nairn (V.C. 89).

I have to thank those who kindly assisted me
in the verification of the specimens, and I would
specially acknowledge my obligations to Mr Wm.
Ingham, B.A., Editor of the " Census Catalogue
of British Mosses," for his valuable notes on many
critical species and varieties.

For the additional good records in the supple-

ment, I have to express my indebtedness to Mr
Magnus Spence, F.E.I.S., Deerness; Mr Robert Tait,
M.O.N.H.S., Stromness; the Rev. D. Lillie, M.A., B.D.,
Watten; the Rev. J. D. Anderson, J.P., Hoy; and
Mr George Ellison, Liverpool. For many interesting
plants I have to thank Mr James Matches, Stromness;
Capt. J. S. Rae, J.P., Stromness; Mr William M'Kay,
J.P., F.E.I.S., Finstown; Mr Dan. Coghill, Stenness;
Miss Kate Thomson, Rackwick; Miss Christina
Clouston, Sunnydale, Stromness; and Mr James
Mowat, Hoy.

J. GRANT.

STROMNESS, *8th September 1913.*

LIST OF ORKNEY MOSSES.

I.—SPHAGNACEÆ.

1 SPHAGNUM, Dill.

A.--CYMBIFOLIA.

1 Cymbifolium, Ehrh.   Common.

β congestum, Schp.   Stenness.
γ pallescens.   Stenness.

2 medium, Limpr.   Hoy.
3 papillosum, Lindb.

β confertum = v. normale.   Hoy.
γ sublæve, Limpr.   Hoy.

B.—TRUNCATA.

5 rigidum v. compactum, De Cand.   Brinkie's Brae, Stromness.

C.—SUBSECUNDA.

6 tenellum, Ehrh.   Brinkie's Brae, Stromness.

β robustum, forma, W. I.   Brinkie's Brae.
γ suberecta, forma, W. I.   Brinkie's Brae.

7 subsecundum, Nees. Stromness.

β contortum, Schp.
γ turgidum, C.M. Loons, Stromness.
δ viride = s. inundatum, Warnst. Loons.
ε viride = s. rufescens. Loons.
ς viride, Boul. Loons.

D.—ACUTIFOLIA.

10 squarrosum, Pers. Loons.
12 acutifolium, Ehrh. Loons.

β subnitens, Dixon. Hoy.
γ rubellum, Russ.
δ rubellum v. rubrum. Stenness.
ε flavo-rubellum. Hoy.
ς robustum, Russ. Stenness.
η violaceum. Hoy
θ virescens. Stenness.
ι pallescens. Stenness.

13 Girgensohnii, Russ. Stenness.
14 fimbriatum, Wils. Stenness and Hoy.
18 cuspidatum, Ehrh.

β falcatum, Russ. Stromness.
γ plumosum, Nees and Hornsch. Rackwick.
δ recurvum v. mucronatum. Burn, Leigh, Stenness.

II.—ANDREÆACEÆ.

2 ANDREÆA, Ehrh.

19 petrophila, Ehrh. Hoy.

IV.—POLYTRICHACEÆ.

4 CATHARINEA, Ehrh.

26 undulata, Web. and Mohr.

Lt.-Colonel J. GRANT, L.R.C.P. & S. Edin.

5 OLIGOTRICHUM, De Cand.

   30 hercynicum, Lam. Græmsay.

6 POLYTRICHUM, Dill.

   31 nanum, Neck.
   32 aloides, Hedw.
      β Dicksoni, Wallm. Brinkie's Brae.
   33 urnigerum, L.
   34 alpinum, L. Loons.
   36 piliferum, Schreb.
   37 juniperum, Willd.
   38 strictum, Banks. Shipyard, Holms, Strom-
      ness.
   40 formosum, Hedw.
   41 commune, L.

VI.—DICRANACEÆ.

10 PLEURIDIUM, Brid.

   46 axillare, Lindb. Burn, Deepdale.
   47 subulatum, Rabenh.

11 DITRICHUM, Timm.

   52 homomallum, Hampe.
   55 flexicaule, Hampe.

16 CERATODON, Brid.

   67 purpureus, Brid.

19 DICHODONTIUM, Schp.

   80 flavescens, Lindb. Garson Burn.

I

21 DICRANELLA, Schp.

    82 heteromalla, Schp.
    83 cerviculata, Schp. Loons, Stromness.
    84 crispa, Schp.   Very rare ; Oglaby bog, Stromness.
    85 secunda, Lindb. Brinkie's Brae.
    87 rufescens, Schp.
    88 varia, Schp.
    91 squarrosa, Schp. Stenness and Hoy.

22 BLINDIA, B. & S.

    93 acuta, B. & S. Stromness.

24 CAMPYLOPUS, Brid.

    96 subulatus, Schp. Very rare ; Stenness and Stromness.
    99 flexuosus, Brid.
    101 fragilis, B. & S.
    104 atrovirens, De Not.
        β muticus, Milde. Very rare ; Petertown, Orphir.
        γ falcatus, Braith. Stromness.
    106 brevipilus, B. & S. Brinkie's Brae.
        β auriculatus, Ferg. Brinkie's Brae.

26 DICRANUM, Hedw.

    116 Bonjeani.
        β calcareum, Braith. Skating Pond, Stromness.
    117 scoparium, Hedw.
        β orthophyllum. Approaches 117 β, Dixon. Brinkie's Brae.
        δ spadiceum, Boul.
        ϵ paludosum, Schp. Loons.

118 majus, Turn.　Garson Burn, Stromness.
119 fuscescens, Turn.　Skating Pond, Stromness.

27 LEUCOBRYUM, Hampe.

128 glaucum, Schp.　Stromness and Hoy.

VII.—FISSIDENTACEÆ.

28 FISSIDENS, Hedw.

135 bryoides, Hedw.
140 osmundoides, Hedw.　Hoy.
143 adiantoides, Hedw.
144 decipiens, De Not.　Stenness.

VIII.—GRIMMIACEÆ.

30 GRIMMIA, Ehrh.

147 apocarpa, Hedw.
　　β rivularis, W. & H.　Garson Burn, Stromness.
　　γ gracilis, Web. & Mohr.　Garson Burn, Stromness.
149 maritima, Turn.
155 pulvinata, Smith.
157 trichophylla, Grev.　Brinkie's Brae.

31 RHACOMITRIUM, Brid.

179 aciculare, Brid.
181 fasciculare, Brid.
182 heterostichum, Brid.
185 lanuginosum, Brid.
186 canescens, Brid.
　　β ericoides, B. & S.

33 PTYCHOMITRIUM, B. & S.

  188 polyphyllum, Furn.   Brownstown, Stromness.

IX.—TORTULACEÆ.

39 POTTIA, Ehrh.

  198 recta, Mitt. Hoy.
  199 bryoides, Mitt.
  200 Heimii, Furnr.
  201 truncatula, Lindb.

40 TORTULA, Hedw.

  225 muralis, Hedw.
  227 subulata, Hedw.
  233 ruralis, Ehrh. Hoy.
  234 ruraliformis, Dixon. Hoy.

41 BARBULA, Hedw. (emend Lindb.)

  239 rubella, Mitt.
  240 tophacea, Mitt. Stenness and Stromness.
     β acutifolia, Schp. Stenness.
  241 fallax, Hedw.
  243 spadicea, Mitt.
  244 rigidula, Mitt. Stromness.
  245 cylindrica, Schp.
  250 Hornschuchiana, Mitt. Pier, Ness, Stromness ; V.C. 96 next station.
  251 revoluta, Brid.
  252 convoluta, Hedw.
  253 unguiculata, Hedw.

42 Leptodontium, Hampe.

255 flexifolium, Hampe.

43 Weisia, Hedw.

266 viridula, Hedw.
267 mucronata, B. & S.
270 rupestris, C.M.
272 verticillata, Brid.   Seashore, pier, Hoy.

44 Trichostomum, B. & S., *emend.*

274 mutabile, Bruch.
277 flavovirens, Bruch.
280 tortuosum, Dixon.

X.—ENCALYPTACEÆ.

47 Encalypta, Schreb.

286 vulgaris (?), Hedw. ⎱ Stromness, indetermin-
288 rhabdocarpa (?)   ⎰   able, without fruit.
289 streptocarpa, Hedw.   Bridge, Stairwaddy.

XI.—ORTHOTRICHACEÆ.

49 Zygodon, Hook. & Taylor.

292 Mougeotii, B. & S.
293 viridissimus, R. Brown.
294 Stirtoni, Schp.   Garth Burn, Stromness.

50 Ulota, Mohr.

299 Drummondi, Brid.   Hoy.
301 crispa, Brid.   Hoy ; Sandy Loch.
303 phyllantha, Brid.

51 ORTHOTRICHUM, Hedw.

305 rupestre, Schleich.
312 affine, Schrad.　Stenness.
318 tenellum, Bruch.　Stenness.
320 diaphanum, Schrad.

55 TETRAPLODON, B. & S.

327 mnioides, B. & S.　Hoy and Stenness.

XIV.—FUNARIACEÆ.

62 FUNARIA, Schreb.

343 fascicularis, Schp.
344 ericetorum, Dixon.　Stromness Harbour.
346 calcarea, Wahl.　Westfield, Stromness.
347 hygrometrica, Sibth.

XV.—MEESIACEÆ.

66 AULACOMNIUM, Schwaeg.

352 palustre, Schwaeg.

XVII.—BARTRAMIACEÆ.

70 BARTRAMIA, Hedw.

360 ithyphylla, Brid.　Hoy and Stenness.

71 PHILONOTIS, Brid.

365 fontana, Brid.
368 seriata, Mitt.　Bog west of Garson Burn,
　　　　and Hoy.　Very rare.
369 calcarea, Schp.　Westfield, Stromness.

72 BREUTELIA, Schp.

  371 arcuata, Schp.

XVIII.—BRYACEÆ.

75 LEPTOBRYUM, Wils.

  374 pyriforme, Wils. Hoy.

76 WEBERA, Hedw.

  379 nutans, Hedw.

      β microphyllum, J. G. (verified by Wm. Ingham).
      Stromness ; only known station.

  381 annotina, Schwaeg.
  386 carnea, Schp. Hoy.
  387 albicans, Schp.

78 BRYUM, Dill.

B.—PTYCHOSTOMUM.

  393 pendulum, Sch. Hoy.

C.—CLADODIUM.

  401 inclinatum.

D.—LEUCODONTIUM.

  404 pallens, S.W.
  406 Duvalii, Voit. Hoy.

E.—EUBRYUM.

  409 pseudo-triquetrum, Schwaeg.
  411 affine, Lindb. Stenness.
  412 pallescens (?). Doubtful, without fruit.

414 caespiticium, L.

416 capillare, L.

419 erythrocarpum, Schwaeg.   Loons, Stromness.

421 atropurpeum, Web. & Mohr.   North End,
        Stromness.

423 alpinum, Huds.   Brinkie's Brae, Stromness.

428 argenteum, L.   North   End,   Stromness
        harbour.

F.—RHODOBRYUM.

79 MNIUM, L. (*emend,* B. & S.)

430 affine, Blaud.   Bog, Garson Burn.

431 cuspidatum, Hedw.

432 rostratum, Schrad.   Outertown, Stromness.

433 undulatum, L.

434 hornum, L.

436 serratum, Schraed.

443 punctatum, L.

444 subglobosum.   Bog, Oglaby, Stromness.

XIX.—FONTINALACEÆ,

81 FONTINALIS, Dill.

446 antipyretica, L.   Burn,   Mooseland ;   and
        Deerness (M. Spence).

XXI.—NECKERACEÆ.

83 NECKERA, Hedw.

456 complanata, Hubn.   Hoy.

84 HOMALIA, Brid.

457 trichomanoides, B. & S.   Græmsay.

XXII.—HOOKERIACEÆ.

87 PTERYGOPHYLLUM, Brid.

460 lucens, Brid.   Seagoe, Hoy.

XXIII.—LEUCODONTACEÆ.

93 POROTRICHUM, Brid.

466 alopecurum, Mitt.   Græmsay and Hoy.

XXXIV.—LESKEACEÆ.

101 THUIDIUM, B. & S.

487 tamariscinum, B. & S.

XXV.—HYPNACEÆ.

102 CLIMACIUM, Web. & Mohr.

491 dendroides, Web. & Mohr.   Bog west of
mouth of Garson Burn.

β depauperata, Boulay.   Fallow field west of
Scarr Cot House, Stenness.   It is found in
only two other stations in the British Isles
(W. Ingham).   Var. is inland, and type
near the seashore in Orkney.—J. G.

103 CYLINDROTHECIUM, B. & S.

492 concinnum, Schp.   Stromness.

107 CAMPTOTHECIUM, B. & S.

497 sericeum, Kindb.
498 lutescens, B. & S.

108 BRACHYTHECIUM, B. & S.

502 albicans, B. & S.
503 salebrosum, v. palustre.　Quarry, Græmsay.
　　　V.C. 107 next station.
504 rutabulum, B. & S.
505 rivulare, B. & S.
511 populeum, B. & S.
512 plumosum, B. & S.　Hoy.
515 purum, Dixon.

109 HYOCOMIUM, B. & S.

516 flagellare, B. & S.　Skating Pond, Stromness.

110 EURHYNCHIUM, B. & S. (*emend* Mille).

518 piliferum, B. & S.
519 crassinervium, B. & S.　Brinkie's Brae.
521 praelongum, Hobk.
　　　β Stokesii, Brid.　Shipbuilding yard ; Garson
　　　　farm.　Next station, V.C. 108.
522 Swartzii, Hobk.　Garson Burn.
524 pumilum, Schp.　Hoy.
527 tenellum, Milde.　Hoy.
528 myosuroides, Schp.
529 myurum, Dixon.
532 striatum, B. & S.
535 rusciforme, Milde.
536 murale, Milde.　Stromness.
537 confertum, Milde.　Stromness.

112 PLAGIOTHECIUM, B. & S.

543 elegans, Sull.　Garson Burn.

549 denticulatum, B. & S.   Hoy.
550 silvaticum, B. & S.   Garson Burn.
551 undulatum, B. & S.   Stromness.

113 AMBLYSTEGIUM, B. & S.

556 serpens, B. & S.   Hoy.
557 Juratzkanum, Schp.   Ness Pier, Stromness.
   Next station, V.C. 89.
560 irriguum, B. & S.   Very rare.   Stromness.
562 filicinum, De Not.

114 HYPNUM, L. (*emend, B. & S.*)

A.—CAMPYLIUM.

564 riparium, L.   Garson Burn.   Next station,
   V.C. 105.
567 stellatum, Schreb.
   β protensum, Rohl.

B.—HARPIDIUM.

571 aduncum, Hedw., now L.
574 lycopodioides, Schwaeg.   Garson Burn ; next
   station, V.C. 90.
575 fluitans, L.
   β Jeanbernati, Ren.   Flotta.
   γ gracile, Boul.   Loons, Stromness.
576 exannulatum, Gumb.
   β brachydictyon, Ren.
   γ pinnatum, forma.   Loons, Stromness.
577 uncinatum, Hedw.
   β plumosum, forma.   Stairwaddy, Stromness.
579 revolvens, Swartz.   Loons.
   forma viride.   Loons.

581 commutatum, Hedw.   Garson Burn.
582 falcatum, Brid.

C.—DREPANIUM.

585 cupressiforme, L.

β resupinatum, Schp.
γ ericetorum, B. & S.
δ elatum, B. & S.

595 molluscum, Hedw.

β condensatum. Schp.   Hoy.
γ robustum, Boul.   Stromness.

D.—LIMNOBIUM.

597 palustre, Huds.
602 ochraceum, Turn.
603 scorpioides, L.
604 stramineum, Dicks.   Brinkie's Brae.
607 cordifolium, Hedw.   Garson Burn.
608 giganteum, Schp.   Bog, Garson Burn.
609 sarmentosum, Wahl.   Bog, Brinkie's Brae.
610 cuspidatum, L.
611 Schreberi, Willd.

115 HYLOCOMIUM, B. & S.

612 splendens, B. & S.
615 brevirostre.   Miffia, Stromness.
616 loreum, B. & S.
617 squarrosum, B. & S.
618 triquetrum, B. & S.

SUPPLEMENT AND SOURCES OF RECORDS.

120 DICRANUM SCOTTIANUM, Turn. Hoy (Rev. D. Lillie, Watten).

319 ORTHOTRICHUM PULCHELLUM, Smith. Deerness (Mr Magnus Spence, Deerness).

352 AULACOMNIUM PALUSTRE, Schwaeg.
> β imbricatum, *forma*, B. & S. Stromness (Mr Robert Tait, Stromness).

526 EURHYNCIUM TEESDALEI, Schp. Hoy (Rev. D. Lillie, Watten).

550 PLAGIOTHECIUM SILVATICUM.
Var. orthocladum, B. & S. Hoy (Rev. J. D. Anderson, Hoy).

585 HYPNUM CUPRESSIFORME.
Var. filiforme, Brid. Binscarth wood (Mr George Ellison, Liverpool).

ADDITIONS BY DR J. GRANT, STROMNESS.

434 MNIUM HORNUM, *forma* Orcadensis, J.G. Garson Burn.

Mr Ingham, under date 6th August 1909, reports with reference to the distinctive points of this plant: —" I have not seen two setæ in one perichætium before. It is very interesting."

504 BRACHYTHECIUM RUTABULUM.
Var. densum. Bank of road, west side of Garson farm-house, Stromness (10th March 1914.)

K

SUPPLEMENT TO FLORA ORCADENSIS.

*T*HIS supplement has been rendered necessary owing to the amount of valuable botanical work done during the summer and autumn of 1912 and 1913 by Col. H. H. Johnston, C.B., D.Sc., F.L.S., who has very kindly submitted his list of rare plants and new discoveries to me and allowed me to make use of them at my discretion. I have selected those which give new localities, confirm the discoveries of earlier botanists, and add new species, but especially new varieties, to the list.

It has been suggested to me that I should draw the attention of botanists, proprietors, and lovers of flowers generally to the nefarious practice—very rare, I am glad to say—of digging up rare plants for sale to florists and others. The mere mention of this practice, I feel sure, will be enough to discourage and reduce it to a minimum. When we botanists dig up two or three rare plants for our herbariums, or for experimental work in our gardens, we believe it to be for the good of Science generally, and quite different from wholesale eradication of rare plants for the sake of a trifling gain.

With the exception of the last two plants, specimens of all the species and varieties mentioned in the following list have been collected and preserved by Colonel H. H. Johnston, who has submitted most of them for identification to the expert botanists named, *e.g.*, "Seen by Mr James Groves," &c.

RANUNCULUS BAUDOTII (Godr.)

Seen by Mr James Groves.   In mud at bottom of water in a loch 8 feet above sea-level, Loch of St. Tredwall, Papa Westray (4th September 1913); native.

FUMARIA PURPUREA (Pugsley).

Seen by Mr Ar. Bennett.   In turnip-field, Swanbister, Orphir (27th August 1880); and Brims, Waas, Hoy (4th August 1913); a weed of cultivation.

SPERGULARIA MARGINATA (Kittel).

Seen by Mr Ar. Bennett.   Rare at roadside at seashore, the Ayre between Aith Hope and Long Hope, Waas, Hoy (21st July 1913); and stony ground near top of crags at seashore, Vaval, Westray (21st August 1913).

Trifolium agrarium (Linn.)

Seen by Mr Ar. Bennett.   In hay-field, Lower 'Tween-the-Brecks, Gyre, Orphir (2nd August 1912); not native.

ROSA CANINA (Linn.)

Var. SPHÆRICA (Gren.)   Seen by Mr J. G. Baker. Heathery banks at burn-side, Berriedale Hoy (4th November 1913); native.

ROSA GLAUCA (Vill.)

Var. CREPINIANA (Déségl.) Seen by Mr J. G. Baker. Banks at burn-side, Mill Burn, Stromness (30th Aug. 1912) ; native, rare.

MYRIOPHYLLUM SPICATUM (Linn.)

Seen by Mr Ar. Bennett. Mud at bottom of water in mill-lead, Loch of Saintear, Westray (23rd August 1913); and mud at bottom of Loch of Boardhouse, Birsay (29th September 1913); native at both places.

APIUM INUNDATUM (Reichb. fil.)

In small pool at summit of Gallow Hill near Established Church Manse, South Waas, Hoy (23rd July 1913). Mr Arthur Bennett, to whom specimens were sent, writes : — " *Helosciadium inundatum* (Koch), var. *isophylla* (Sonder), ' Flora of Hamburgh,' p. 158, 1851 "; but this variety is not mentioned in the " London Catalogue," 10th edition.

HEDERA HELIX (Linn.)

Colonel H. H. Johnston says regarding this plant :—" I collected the ivy at Berriedale, Hoy, on 15th May 1884, but on visiting Berriedale on 4th November 1913 I could find no trace of it. Apparently the bank on which I found it in 1884 has been undermined and fallen into the burn."

ARCTIUM NEMOROSUM (Lej.), of Babington's " Manual of British Botany," ninth edition, p. 217 (1904).

Very rare on sandy links near the seashore, Melsetter, Waas, Hoy (11th August 1913) ; and links, Westray (26th August 1913); native at both places.

NOTE.—Mr Arthur Bennett, to whom specimens of the ARCTIUM from Westray were sent, informed Col. H. H. Johnston that the *"Arctium nemorosum* (Lejeune)" of British authors is not the plant of Lejeune ; and that the plants from Orkney are *Arctium vulgare* (A. H. Evans), var. *pycnocephalum* (A. H. Evans), in " Journal of Botany," vol. li., p. 117 (April 1913).

Crepis nicœensis (Balb.)

Seen by Mr Ar. Bennett. In hay-field, Lower 'Tween-the-Brecks, Gyre, Orphir (2nd August 1912) ; a weed of cultivation, not native.

HIERACIUM RUBICUNDUM (F. J. Hanbury).

Seen by Rev. E. F. Linton. Sandstone crags at seashore, west side of Walkmill Bay, Orphir (19th and 20th July 1912); rare on grassy crags, Melsetter, Waas, Hoy (11th August 1913); native at both places.

HIERACIUM CALEDONICUM (F. J. Hanbury).

Seen by Rev. E. F. Linton. Grassy banks at seashore, Scapa, St. Ola (5th July 1912) ; native.

HIERACIUM BUGLOSSOIDES (Arv.-Touv.)

Seen by Rev. E. F. Linton. Crags at seashore, west side of Walkmill Bay, Orphir (15th August 1881); native.

HIERACIUM SCOTICUM (F. J. Hanbury).

Seen by Rev. E. F. Linton. Crags on hill-side, North Hill, Westray (15th July 1883 and 28th August 1913) ; very rare on Vins Hamar, Fitty Hill,

Westray (5th September 1913); crags at burn-side, Sowa Dee, Sandwick (26th August 1912); crags at seashore, east side of Aith Hope, South Waas, Hoy (21st July 1913); and grassy crags at seashore, west side of Aith Hope, Waas, Hoy (4th August 1913); native at all these places.

HIERACIUM SILVATICUM (Gouan.)

Var. TRICOLOR (W. R. Linton). Seen by Rev. E. F. Linton. Crags on hillside 430 feet above sea-level; Dwarfie Hamars, Hoy (22nd July 1912); native.

HIERACIUM ORCADENSE (W. R. Linton).

Seen by Rev. E. F. Linton. Crags on hill-side, Hoy (14th August 1879); Dwarfie Hamars, Hoy (10th August 1886, and 22nd July 1912); and very fine and luxuriant plants on crags at the seashore, west side of Walkmill Bay, Orphir (19th and 20th July 1912); native at all these places. Specimens collected by Col. H. H. Johnston on crags on hill-side, Ward Hill, Hoy, on 18th August 1881, are doubtfully referred to this species by the Rev. E. F. Linton, who states that "the specimens are too poor to name with any certainty."

Col. H. H. Johnston informs me that he got *Pyrola rotundifolia* (Linn.), on a heathery hill-side 320 feet above sea-level, in Hoy (22nd July 1912). He also collected specimens of *Utricularia minor* (Linn.), in the swamp at the foot of the north-north-west slope of Cringla Field just on the Sandwick side of the boundary between the parishes of Sandwick and Stromness, on 26th August 1912.

PRIMULA SCOTICA (Hook.)

Pastures near the sea, Bay of Moclett, Papa Westray (9th September 1913), and sandy pastures at seashore, North Hill, Papa Westray (10th September 1913); native at both places. At the former station the plants had scapes or were acaulescent, and at the latter station all the specimens collected by Col. H. H. Johnston were acaulescent.

TRIENTALIS EUROPÆA (Linn.)

Kingsdale, Firth (9th July 1913); native. Plants were in full bloom. This plant was first found in Orkney at this station in June 1847, by the late Mr George Robson.

GENTIANA CAMPESTRIS (Linn.)

Sandy links at seashore, Links of Melsetter, Waas, Hoy (11th August 1913). Mr Ar. Bennett writes :—" I suppose a state of *G. baltica* (Murbeck), but I am not sure"; and pastures, Point of Huro, Westray (2nd September 1913). Mr Ar. Bennett again writes:—" It is probable that these specimens are *G. baltica* (Murbeck)." The specimens were not in good condition for identification, Colonel H. H. Johnston informs me. *G. baltica* (Murbeck) is a subspecies of *G. campestris* (Linn.)

VERONICA CHAMÆDRYS (Linn.)

Turf wall near Galaha, Smoogro, Orphir (19th July 1912); very rare.

EUPHRASIA OFFICINALIS (Linn.)

This plant has by botanists—especially Townsend

—been recently classified into several species. In my list on p. 52 I have given three varieties, viz., *Rost-koviana, gracilis,* and *maritima.* Colonel H. H. Johnston, C.B., has made several collections of *Euphrasia* and sent them to the Rev. E. S. Marshall for identification, which he named as follow :—

EUPHRASIA BREVIPILA (Burnat & Gremli).

Grassy crags at seashore, east side of Aith Hope, South Waas, Hoy (21st July 1913); native.

EUPHRASIA BOREALIS (Townsend).

Common on grassy and heathery pastures, and native at all the following places :—Stenness (6th August 1875); Binscarth, Firth (21st August 1880); Skaill, Sandwick (19th August 1881); Linksness, Hoy (20th August 1885); The Bout, Veness, Orphir (19th July 1912) ; Black Craig, Stromness (19th August 1912); and Brims, Waas, Hoy (4th August 1913).

EUPHRASIA GRACILIS (Fries).

Common on heaths, and native at all the following places :—Hoy (15th August 1874) ; Waas, Hoy (9th August 1877); Burn of Ore, Waas, Hoy (16th July 1912); Pegal Burn and North Dale, Waas, Hoy (7th August 1912); Brunt Hill, Stromness (23rd August 1912) ; and near Rosehill, Stromness (30th August 1912).

EUPHRASIA SCOTTICA (Wettst.)

Heath on hill-side, North Dale, Waas, Hoy (7th August 1912); native.

EUPHRASIA CURTA (Wettst.)

Pasture at edge of crags at the seashore, Ness of Ramnageo, Sandwick (23rd July 1886); native.

Var. GLABRESCENS (Wettst.)

Common on grassy and heathery pastures, and native at all the following places:—Ward Hill, Hoy (15th August 1912); Burn of Selta, Stromness (19th August 1912); Dale of Oback, Orphir (9th July 1913); and Brims, Waas, Hoy (4th August 1913). ·

EUPHRASIA FOULAENSIS (Townsend).

Short pasture 150 feet above sea level, drenched with sea-spray during storms, Vaval, Westray (21st August 1913); native.

NOTE.—All the above mentioned species and variety of *Euphrasia*, except *E. gracilis*, were found in Mainland, Orkney, in 1900, by the Rev. E. S. Marshall (see *The Journal of Botany*, Vol. xxxix., p. 270, August 1901), and are identical with those found by Col. H. H. Johnston, with the exception of *E. gracilis*.

ATRIPLEX PATULA (Linn.)

Var. ANGUSTIFOLIA (Sm.) Seen by Mr Ar. Bennett. Stony ground near top of crags at seashore, Vaval, Westray (21st August 1913); native.

POTAMOGETON PERFOLIATUS (Linn.)

Var. CORDATO-LANCEOLATUS (Mert. & Koch). Seen by Mr Ar. Bennett. Mud at bottom of Loch of Boardhouse, Birsay (29th Sept. 1913). Leaves were

1½ to 3 inches long, cordato-lanceolate. This variety, Mr Ar. Bennett says, is not the same plant as var. *lanceolatus* (Blytt) in "London Catalogue," 10th Ed., so that this variety is new to British flora, and not previously included in floras.

ELEOCHARIS UNIGLUMIS (Schultes).

Name confirmed by Mr Ar, Bennett. Water channel in marsh near the sea, Myres Bay, South Waas, Hoy (19th July 1913) ; native ; common in the marsh.

CAREX FULVA (Host.) × OEDERI (Retz).

Seen by Mr Ar. Bennett. Pastures at loch side, Loch of Saintear, Westray (23rd August 1913) ; and pastures at loch side, Loch of Swartmill, Westray (6th September 1913) ; native, and very rare at both stations.

NOTE.—This hybrid is not the same as *Carex fulva* (Good.), var. *sterilis*, which Dr Boswell, in "English Botany," 3rd Ed., "rather considers to be a hybrid between *Carex fulva* (Good.) and *Carex flava* (Linn.)"

CAREX EXTENSA (Good.)

Var. MINOR (Syme). Seen by Mr Ar. Bennett. Stony ground near the seashore, North Hill, Westray (28th August 1913) ; native.

CAREX OEDERI (Retz).

Var. ŒDOCARPA (And.) Seen by Mr Ar. Bennett. Stony loch shore, Loch of Kirbister, Orphir (30th June 1913) ; native.

AVENA PRATENSIS (Linn.)

Seen by Mr Ar. Bennett. Very common on sandy links near the seashore, Links of Melsetter, Waas, Hoy (11th August 1913) ; native. Each spikelet has one awn only, whereas Mr Ar. Bennett writes :— "Almost always there are two awns, and sometimes three. All my specimens have at least two. Your plant seems to agree with Nouman's *f. pauciflora*, " Flora Arcticæ Norvegiæ," p. 54, 1893.

GLYCERIA PLICATA (Fries.)

Seen by Mr Ar. Bennett. Marsh, Burn of Ore, Waas. Hoy (29th July 1913) ; native.

AGROPYRON REPENS (Beauv.)

Var. LEERSIANUM (Gray). Seen by Mr Ar. Bennett. Common on shell-sand and shingle at sea-shore, Hookin, Papa Westray (4th September 1913) ; native.

POLYSTICHUM LONCHITIS (Roth.)

Clefts of rocks on hill-side, Ward Hill, Hoy (3rd Oct. 1913); native ; fifteen plants only seen by Col. H. H. Johnston.

CHARA FRAGILIS (Desv.)

Var. CAPILLACEA (Coss. & Germ.) Seen by Mr J. Groves. Shallow pool, Rotten Loch, Brims, Waas, Hoy (4th August 1913); native; common in the pool. Mr J. Groves writes:—" I refer this to var. *capillacea*, but the primary cortical cells are larger than usual." Also in deep water in a quarry, Kirkbrae, Westray (1st September 1913); native ; common in the quarry.

Var. BARBATA (Gant.) Seen by Mr J. Groves. Mud at bottom of stagnant water in a quarry, Berstane, St. Ola (13th September 1913); native.

CHARA ASPERA (Willd.)

Var. SUBINERMIS (Kuetz.) Seen by Mr J. Groves. Mud at bottom of water five feet deep, Loch of Board-house, Birsay (29th September 1913); native; very common in the loch.

MALVA MOSCHATA (Linn.)

Several plants of this species were found in grass land of Greentofts, Deerness, during August of 1913. These showy flowers were in full bloom. They have, no doubt, been brought with seeds, and the lovely summer of that year favoured their fine development.

PARNASSIA PALUSTRIS (Linn.)

Two curious monstrosities of the Grass of Parnassus were brought to me from the Banks of Pool, Deerness, in August 1913. Its single-leaved stem and beautifully pencilled petals left no doubt as to its relationship. It had, however, as far as I could ascertain, only three stamens bearing anthers, and its numerous glands and antherless stamens had developed into petals. All these petals—from 25 to 30—were pencilled with the same graceful lines.

Note on a New Primula found in Orkney by Mr M. Spence.

BY

C. E. MOSS, D.Sc., F.L.S., F.R.G.S.,
Curator of the Herbarium, University of Cambridge.

Three years ago Mr M. Spence sent two forms of *Primula scotica* to Mr E. W. Hunnybun to draw for the "Cambridge British Flora." One of these was quite typical of the form originally described and figured by Hooker in the second edition of the "Flora Londonensis," p. 133 (1819), and calls for no further comment.

The second plant, however, differed, as Mr Spence correctly pointed out, in possessing narrower, less compact, more spathulate, and more obtuse leaves. Its petals also, as Mr Spence rightly stated, were longer, relatively narrower, and more deeply cut. The plant received by Mr Hunnybun was in good flower, and was duly drawn. The plant was grown, and, to Mr Hunnybun's great surprise, developed a capsule which differed from the ordinary form of *P. scotica* in being 1·5 to 2·0 times as long as the calyx. In this respect the plant recalls *P. farinosa*; and if the latter species grew in Orkney, there is no doubt that some botanists would at once have jumped to the conclusion that the new form was a hybrid. However, as *P. farinosa* is not known north of Midlothian, this hypothesis is quite untenable. At first, when Mr Hunnybun drew my attention to the plant, I thought the plant was a connecting link of *P. scoitca* and *P. farinosa*; and I intended to name it *P. scotica* variety *orkniensis* (see "Proceedings Cambridge Philosophic Society," xvii. 255, 1913.)

Further examination, however, tended to throw doubt on this second theory, for I find that Mr Spence's new plant verges towards *P. stricta* (Fries.), a Scandinavian species, and *perhaps is actually this species*. Therefore, before actually naming the plant in view of its possible identity with *P. stricta* (Fries.), I desire to see further material with ripe fruits and seeds. In any case, the discovery is interesting; and it may prove to be important in the sense of adding another species to the British flora.

In the south of England, one finds every year new varieties or species identical with those of western or northern France; and I am of opinion that several new varieties and even species, with Scandinavian affinities, in the extreme north of Scotland still await discovery. I hope, therefore, that Mr Spence's new plant, whatever name it may ultimately be found to bear, will stimulate critical Scottish botanists, and cause them to re-examine their flora in the light of the suggestion here made.

C. E. MOSS.

Cambridge, 28/3/1914.

BIBLIOGRAPHY.

NAME OF WORK.	AUTHOR.	DATE.
List of Orkney Plants in History of Orkney.	Dr James Wallace, M.D., F.R.S.	1700.
List of Orkney Plants in Barry's History of Orkney.	Rev. Geo. Low, Minister of Birsay and Harray.	1774 & after. Published in 1805.
Tour in Orkney with a view chiefly to objects of Natural History.	Mr Patrick Neill, M.A., Secy. to Nat. Hist. Soc. of Edinburgh.	1806.
Flora Orcadensis in Mr H. C. Watson's List MS. at Kew.	Dr Gillies.	Circa 1820.
New Botanists' Guide.	p. 517	1837.
MS. List of all Orkney Plants they had met with.	Dr A. R. Duguid, of Kirkwall. Mr Robert Heddle, Melsetter.	Circa 1850.
Anderson's Guide to the Orkney Islands.	Chas. Clouston, LL.D., Minister of Sandwick.	1862.
Journal of Botany, p. 11.	H. C. Watson, Esq.	1864.
A new List of the Flowering Plants and Ferns of Orkney.	Wm. Irvine Fortescue, Esq. of Swanbister, now Dr Fortescue, of Kincausie.	1879-1880.
English Botany, 3rd edition. Plantago Maritima var hirsuta.		1867.
The Scottish Naturalist.	Vol. V., pp. 318, 362, pp. 26, 72.	1881-1882. 1883-1884.

Name of Work.	Author.	Date.
ions to Flora of Ork-. Annals Scot. Nat. t.	Col. H. H. Johnston, D.Sc., F.L.S., F.R.S.E. p. 173.	1895.
on Lepidopitra ob- ed during a short anical Tour in Orkney Zetland.	F. J. Hanbury, Esq.	1895.
y Records. Journal Botany.	Vol. XXI. pp. 20,21,279,288,352. pp 2, 5, 29, 217, 235. p. 377.	1883. 1884. 1886.
ctions. Annals of t. Nat. Hist.	Col. H. H. Johnston, D.Sc.,F.R.S.,C.B., F.R.S.E p. 252.	1904.
on Juncus Effusus var alis. Transactions . Soc., Edinburgh.	Mr Magnus Spence	1906.
irtium Palustra in Ork-. Annals of Scot. . Hist.	Mr Arthur Bennett, F.L.S., p. 54.	1908.
ions to Flora of ney.	Mr Arthur Bennett, F.L.S.	1909.
Grassland of Orkney : Æcological Analysis.	MrG.W.Scarth,M.A., Assist. to Prof. of Botany, Edinb'gh.	1911.
sh Forms of Sper- um in Scottish Botan- Review.	Mr Arthur Bennett, F.L.S.	1912.
aga aizoides, Hoy, ney, in Scottish Bo- ical Review.	Mr Arthur Bennett, F.L.S.	1912
nogeton praelongus in ney, in Scottish Re- v.	Mr Arthur Bennett, F.L.S.	1912.

INDEX.

(The names of varieties and synonyms are in italics.)

WM. PEACE & SON, PRINTERS, KIRKWALL.

SD - #0034 - 080324 - C0 - 229/152/15 - PB - 9781314824032 - Gloss Lamination